TWENTIETH CENTURY INTERPRETATIONS
OF

JULIUS CAESAR

A Collection of Critical Essays

Edited by
LEONARD F. DEAN

10/24/69

Prentice-Hall, Inc. A SPECTRUM BOOK *Englewood Cliffs, N. J.*

 Library of Congress Catalog Card Number 69-11355. Printed in the United States of America.

Current printing (last number):
10 9 8 7 6 5 4 3 2 1

Prentice-Hall International, Inc. (*London*)

Contents

TWENTIETH CENTURY INTERPRETATIONS

OF

JULIUS CAESAR

Introduction

by Leonard F. Dean

Because of its use in the schools, *Julius Caesar* is one of the best known of Shakespeare's plays, and yet it has not generally been talked about as a play. It probably got into the curriculum to begin with for institutional rather than dramatic reasons: the best possible English substitute for Latin, gives practice in public speaking, not sexy, easily cast in a boys' school, and so on. It apparently meant a great deal to nineteenth-century critics, but they thought of it not so much as a play as a collection of biographies, particularly of Brutus, an aristocrat whom they could praise and patronize at the same time. Here is a small sample from Edward Dowden, one of the best of his time (1872):

> In *Julius Caesar,* Shakespeare makes a complete imaginative study of a man predestined to failure, who nevertheless retains to the end the moral integrity which he prized as his highest possession, and who with each new error advances a fresh claim upon our admiration and our love. . . . The life of Brutus, as the lives of such men must be, was a good life, in spite of its disastrous fortunes. He had found no man who was not true to him. And he had known Portia. . . . No relation of man and woman in the plays of Shakespeare is so altogether noble. . . . The love of Brutus could not be given except with admiration equal to his love. . . . Portia, while perfectly a woman, must be to him more than a woman; she must be an ideal of august and adorable heroism.

Twentieth-century interpretations of *Julius Caesar* have been in part a response to the nineteenth century. An early reaction to the view represented by Dowden and others was to stand it on its head. Thus Mark Van Doren, thirty years ago, described Brutus as a stuffed shirt and a wind bag, and there have been many later variations on this theme. Another early reaction was to take a worldly, rather than a moral view of the play. John Palmer[1] (1945) is particularly knowledge-

[1] See pp. 17–20.

able about the Deciuses of politics, the typical junior minister, who "sounds an echo, through the ages, of pleasantries exchanged in antechambers, lobbies, corridors, or other purlieus where little people attend their masters." Antony is similarly recognizable as a type to Harley Granville-Barker[2] (1927, 1946):

> though we may father him on Plutarch, to English eyes there can be no more typically English figure than the sportsman turned statesman, but sportsman still. . . . Nor has Shakespeare any illusions as to what the harsher needs of politics may convert your sportsman once he is out to kill.

But again the emphasis is not on the play as a play.

The late Leo Kirschbaum was among the first, characteristically, to turn away from nineteenth-century critical topics toward the variety of fresh approaches to be found in recent criticism of *Caesar*. Twenty years ago he complained that the leading critics, from Van Doren and Granville-Barker back to the eighteenth century, seemed to be responding to something cleaner and more literary than the bloody play actually on the stage. Kirschbaum wanted to remind us that the Elizabethan stage went in for strong theatrical effects, and that our divine William, as a working Elizabethan dramatist, was not too nice for blood. There is no denying that *Julius Caesar* is theatrical in this sense. It shows what great men do at work. They plot, make inflammatory speeches, and kill each other. It is a violent and bloody business.

Julius Caesar is also a product of the Elizabethan stage in another sense. The theatrical vitality of Elizabethan drama is demonstrated by its kaleidoscopic variety of dramatic modes, forms, and devices. One may call it experimental or undisciplined, but never tame. The astonishing mixture of modes and forms in Marlowe's plays, for example, may or may not be related to mixed feelings on his part about the Establishment, but it certainly illustrates the fact that as a playwright he was never timid or proper. Item: What would be the effects of presenting a King as Retarded Child (Mycetes), or as Homosexual Aesthete (Edward II)? Item: Can farce become a stage metaphor for the unremitting madness of respectable machiavellianism (*The Jew of Malta*)? Item: What do you make of the undertone of soap opera in heroic drama? ("But tell me, madam, is your grace betrothed?" 'One thing you can say for Tamburlaine, he had good manners. He always asked a girl if she was engaged before he went any farther.') The

[2] See pp. 21–26.

moral, for playwrights, is that one way to be lucky is to get into trouble. John Marston illustrates this better than a genius like Marlowe. One of Marston's weaknesses was a tendency to notice that his own serious characters might suddenly look comic, and this forced him into improvising some of his best scenes, moments, for example, when we find ourselves tiptoeing gingerly around important, Brutus-like figures as we act out the naughty-boy feeling that these big fellows are hard to handle, any word may set them off. *Julius Caesar* is Elizabethan and theatrical in this sense as well as in its blood and violence.

An emphatic way to make the point is to say that the theatricality of *Caesar* is so great that it often seems to be unsupervised, as if Shakespeare were at two removes from the stage and were putting on his play by letting his characters put on plays of their own. Everybody seems to be in on some act, as player, director, or writer. When the play opens, the director-tribunes are reprimanding the citizens for misplaying their parts. Two political playlets sponsored by Caesar follow, but they are subordinated to a major political show being cast by Cassius. This in turn is rapidly taken over by the star, Brutus, who makes it into an old-fashioned patriotic drama, which he feels will have many re-runs. It is in fact closed abruptly. Antony's servant enters and announces a change in the program. "Brutus is noble, wise, valiant, and honest; Caesar was mighty, bold, royal, and loving." Okay, so what's new? That was your show; now watch the next star. And Antony, by contrast, is certainly modern: knowing, easily colloquial, and endlessly skillful at playing up to whatever is in the changing air. The problem is to know what all this seemingly unsupervised theatricality means. How are we to take it and the characters who put it on? The few scenes which seem to be put on by Shakespeare directly, as it were, are those whose purposes and effects are quite clear. The most famous is the quarrel between Brutus and Cassius. It is a beautifully efficient exercise in psychological realism and self-exposure. This scene has never puzzled anyone, and it would grace any problem play. Elsewhere the effects may be confused, contradictory, or apparently unintended, and therefore controversial.

It is the imperfectly controlled theatricality of the play, for example, that makes even the leading roles seem at times to be character parts, and when heroes are squeezed into character parts, a wayward comic effect is produced. With me this takes the form of an irresistible temptation to think of Brutus as Pistol. And a good case can be made for the resemblance, along the lines of Ann Righter's fine description of

Pistol as a one-man play within the play who comes from God knows where with his old-fashioned stage talk and his exalted emotions. It is as impossible to communicate with Brutus as with Pistol; at least Brutus never really hears or seriously considers the practical proposals made to him. His characteristic response is to brush them off, almost automatically, and then deliver a speech in his own language. "No, not an oath," and so on. Antony, who has some of Falstaff's linguistic range, comes closest to being able to communicate with Brutus, and his final eulogy may be simply an appropriate exercise in Brutus-talk. Of course Pistol is safely confined in a comic context, which tells us how to take him, even though he is bewilderingly stagy. We take a cue from Falstaff and become fond of the unquenchable Pistolian spirit behind the abnormality of speech. The unquenchable spirit of Brutus is more confusing. It should be noble rather than comic, and either way the theatricality soon leads to blood. When Brutus displaces Cassius as the director of the plot, the oratorical mind begins to resemble the computer mind. It uses language in a way that seems inhuman. It speaks of killing the spirit of Caesar separately from the body, so that the assassination will be cost-effective. If it is questioned, it oratorically implies that the subject is closed, and the tone therefore becomes self-congratulatory. Oratory is the right speech for that protected, old-fashioned, heroic place from which Brutus seems to have come when he enters the play. There nobility is disembodied and uncolored by circumstances, and it is consequently a proper subject for oratorical celebration, like flowers. But here and now in the play, the oratorical becomes theatrical, the eloquent hero contracts into a stage type, and the type in turn acquires a nightmarish reality as it irresistibly acts out the stunted logic of its being. Did Shakespeare intend this? Did he mean to undermine the nobility of Brutus? Is this controlled or accidental?

Another subject which is confused by the theatricality of the play is the relation between the citizens and the aristocrats. Why do the two groups have to pay attention to each other? Do Caesar, Brutus, or Antony really need to get the support of the people? Why after a change of power is it necessary to explain to the citizens what has happened? When Shakespeare returns to Rome seven years later in *Coriolanus,* questions like these are firmly and clearly related to the character of the hero, to his special integrity. The play defines that integrity as an instinctive, even violent insistence that there is no necessary or essential connection between the aristocrats and the citizens, that the fable of the belly and the members with its ideal of mutuality is not warranted by the facts, that electioneering is immoral, and that aristocrats everywhere, Roman or Volscian, are completely independent and self-contained. Coriolanus' integrity is one effective solution to the credibility gap. Honesty is the opposite of democracy. But in *Julius Caesar,* where everyone is always on stage, the relation between ruler and ruled is obscure or is as intricate as that between actor and audience. Why do they need each other? And what does honesty mean in the theater?

An attempt to answer questions like these points again toward the central critical problem of the play, a problem that becomes acute in the last act. Crudely stated, that problem is a lack of cooperation or an opposition between the meaning conveyed by the theatrical forms and the meaning conveyed by the other elements of the play. A dominant theatrical form in the last act is the Roman suicide, with appropriate accompanying comment on life and death. This piece of theater has a built-in message which says, unless it is controlled, that something vaguely noble is happening. Other elements in the play say, on the contrary, that something stupid, cynical, or ironically disastrous is happening. Shakespeare was not lucky in the last act, and he was careful not to get into this particular trouble again. When Horatio threatens to be an "antique Roman," Hamlet wrests the cup from his hand and orders him back to the living theme of the play; and Cleopatra's suicide in the "high Roman fashion" is in truth, of course, her greatest Egyptian act.

Even Shakespeare had to learn how to handle Rome, with its accumulation of stock meanings and ready-made theatricality. He may have absorbed many of the clichés of Roman history at the Stratford grammar school (certainly the Elizabethan curriculum exhibits the taste normal to officials concerned with the moral character of the young), but it was in the London theater, where he was well established by the time he was twenty-eight, that he learned how indispensable a conventional knowledge of the past is to the dramatist. By the time of *Caesar* (1599–1600), he had written the nine plays based on English history that make him our greatest historical dramatist. Those plays are firmly grounded on the stereotypes of popular history—good and bad kings, wise old counselors, flattering parasites, wayward princes, and so on, as well as on the special simplifications of Tudor propaganda. Against this ground of clichés it was possible to conduct a creative criticism or exploration by appropriately theatrical means, of which Falstaff is simply the most dazzling example. The same opportunity existed with Roman history. The amalgam of tones and modes in *Julius Caesar* is full of possibilities, but they are not clearly and effectively realized. The next year Shakespeare went on to *Hamlet*, and then to the problem plays and the great tragedies. When he returned to Rome in 1606–8, the wild possibilities which had existed in *Caesar* are contracted into the hard outlines of Coriolanus and Octavius, and finally, "barber'd ten times o'er," we leave Rome on a theatrical exploration of an older stereotype, the Siren of the Nile, who beckons from her chaise longue, while kneeling handmaidens busy themselves with rare unguents and dimpled native boys wave their plumed fans in the soft air.

Julius Caesar, despite its blood and violence and its air of containing plays within plays, is unexpectedly deficient in a range of experience and feeling that we associate with Cleopatra precisely because of her extraordinary theatricality. This range includes the proverbial vulgarity of show business, the kind of thing that Shakespeare pointed to painfully in his lines on motley and the dyer's hand and that worried Groucho Marx in his meeting with T. S. Eliot. It includes not only histrionics, tantrums and a general lack of decorum, but also the "vilest things" that, as Enobarbus reports, were miraculously becoming in Cleopatra. It includes the energy that respectable categories, like Roman "whore" for Cleopatra, are unable to contain. It includes the sheer bad taste which is a vital part of Egypt, or of such a wildly theatrical play as *The Jew of Malta*: the crude insistence on the big nose, the repeated stale jokes about hanky-panky in the convent, the old gags and routines, the coarse indifference to proper feelings and adequate motivation. The histrionics of Richard III are similarly vulgar, an expression of contempt for all the claims of decency and order. Falstaff, the greatest of actors, is more complex, but among other things he is also a sleazy entertainer whose occupational disrespect for the gentry can always be counted on, as it ranges from the extreme of radical skepticism to behavior which is simply unbecoming in an older man. On a smaller scale it is equally natural that the furiously theatrical Pistol should be pleased to think of his heroic king in cheap music-hall terms as a "lovely bully."

In *Julius Caesar,* however, this natural tendency of the theatrical to open into vulgarity is curiously aborted. Antony does show promising signs of developing a flashy second-rate side to his character, Caesar does contain the makings of a stagy eccentric, the outlines of a compulsively comic orator are visible in Brutus; but none of this is seemingly free to develop. It is rounded off, as we say, and thus the play lacks much of the lower register, the range which distinguishes a major work from a lesser one.

The feeling that the Elizabethans did their best thinking in and through the theater reflects the idea that theatrical "thought" is bigger than academic thought, that it goes beyond logic and polite learning and received value to include the illogical, the irrational, and the vulgar. Perhaps *Julius Caesar* really is a school play. Or rather was a school play, because the schools and their social role have changed. An English class in present-day England is likely to be a dramatic happening set up to engage vulgar energies and incite theatrical "thinking." In this new situation, *Julius Caesar* lingers on, cut off from its old functions and largely useless. But history has taught us to be humble about deciding that any of Shakespeare's plays are permanently exhausted and dated. The eighteen selections which follow are humble attempts to become re-engaged with the created life of the play.

Julius Caesar

by Mark Van Doren

Shakespeare idealized Plutarch's Brutus, but not in the direction of his own Henry V. The Roman conspirator has become an exemplary gentleman, and the chief sign of this is his set of scruples. His imagination is indeed so selfless, and his consideration of other men so full and kind, as almost to smother his powers and render him inactive. He is not very much like Hamlet, whose inaction, if inaction it is, has its paradoxical dynamics. But he is a sober step in that direction—too sober for the kind of success his creator, with a nimble bound back into the northern scene, is next to achieve.

If Brutus is less interesting than Hamlet, if his internal complications diminish rather than exhibit his dramatic force, the principal reason may be that Shakespeare has kept himself too conscious of a remote Roman grandeur in the scene. In Plutarch he seems always to have recognized an artist whom it would be rash to change, but his respect for the biographer was in the present case perhaps too solemn. The accommodation of his style to an ancient and alien atmosphere is amazingly complete, and there is in *Julius Caesar* a perfection of form which even he will never surpass. But the accommodation is something of a tour de force, and the perfection is of that sort which limits rather than releases poetry. *Julius Caesar* is more rhetoric than poetry, just as its persons are more orators than men. They all have something of the statue in them, for they express their author's idea of antiquity rather than his knowledge of life. They have the clarity and simplicity of worked marble, and are the easiest of Shakespeare's people to understand if one expects everything from speeches, and if one is innocent of the distinction between men and public men. The characters of *Julius Caesar* are public men. Even Antony and Caesar are. But Shakespeare's deepest interest is in the private man. And though he

---

tries to find that man in Brutus he does not do so, because he has already submitted Brutus, like everybody else in the play, to the smoothing and simplifying process of a certain style. This style is in its way wonderful, but the hero who follows Brutus will accomplish infinitely greater wonders in no style at all, or at any rate in none that can be named; unless its name is Shakespeare's English.

Julius Caesar is least notable among Shakespeare's better plays for the distinctions of its speech. All of its persons tend to talk alike; their training has been forensic and therefore uniform, so that they can say anything with both efficiency and ease. With Marullus's first speech in the opening scene the play swings into its style: a style which will make it appear that nobody experiences the least difficulty in saying what he thinks. The phrasing is invariably flawless from the oral point of view; the breathing is right; no thought is too long for order or too short for roundness. Everything is brilliantly and surely said; the effects are underlined, the i's are firmly dotted. Speeches have tangible outlines, like plastic objects, and the drift from one of them to another has never to be guessed, for it is clearly stated.

The characters are accomplished in all the practical arts of statement. Not merely in the Forum is Brutus an orator—"I pause for a reply" (III, ii, 37)—but in his private tent, quarreling with Cassius. Dryden admired the famous quarrel scene (IV, iii) because it was "masculine," and his admiration was sound; yet the epithet implies a limitation of effect. The thump and rap of the repartee remind us once more that public men are training their tongues against each other; the dialogue, for all its power, could do with some relief by way of things half said or never said. Brutus and Cassius say it all—with knowledge, too, of how it will be taken. Along with the rest here they are artists in declamation.

Rhetorical questions abound in *Julius Caesar.*

> Wherefore rejoice? What conquest brings he home?
> What tributaries follow him to Rome
> To grace in captive bonds his chariot-wheels? . . .
> And do you now put on your best attire?
> And do you now cull out a holiday?
> And do you now strew flowers in his way
> That comes in triumph over Pompey's blood? (I, i, 37–56)

There they are piled in parallel formation, and this is frequently the case. Antony knows best the trick of letting them forth singly, with the force of simple assertion:

> Did this in Caesar seem ambitious? (III, ii, 95)

> You will compel me, then, to read the will? (III, ii, 161)

Portia, the public wife of a public man, goes so far as to answer one of hers:

> Is Brutus sick? . . .
> No, my Brutus;
> You have some sick offence within your mind.
> (II, i, 261–68)

But all in these various ways know how to ask them, and how not to pause for a reply unless the pause too will be effective.

So are they tutored in the music of monosyllables. No play of Shakespeare's has so many, so superbly used. The seasoned orator strings short words together as often as he can—for an effect of artlessness, of sincerity that only speaks right on, and also because there is a secret pleasure in demonstrating the discipline of his tongue. It takes skill to deliver monosyllables in an agreeable and natural rhythm, and a rhetorician likes nothing better than problems of skill. In *Julius Caesar* there may be in one place as many as thirty monosyllables together.

> And when the fit was on him, I did mark
> How he did shake—'t is true, this god did shake. (I, ii, 120–21)

> When went there by an age, since the great flood,
> But it was fam'd with more than with one man?
> When could they say, till now, that talk'd of Rome . . .
> (I, ii, 152–54)

> I will come home to you; or, if you will,
> Come home to me, and I will wait for you.
> I will do so; till then, think of the world. (I, ii, 309–11)

> What's to do?
> A piece of work that will make sick men whole.
> But are not some whole that we must make sick? (II, i, 326–28)

> Let me know some cause,
> Lest I be laugh'd at when I tell them so.
> The cause is in my will; I will not come. (II, ii, 69–71)

> If thou dost bend and pray and fawn for him,
> I spurn thee like a cur out of my way. (III, i, 45–46)

'T is good you know not that you are his heirs;
For, if you should, O, what would come of it! (III, ii, 150–51)

I pray you, sirs, lie in my tent and sleep;
It may be I shall raise you by and by. . . .
I will not have it so: lie down, good sirs. . . .
I know young bloods look for a time of rest. . . .
I will not hold thee long. If I do live,
I will be good to thee. (IV, iii, 246–66)

They may occur in orations or they may crop out in discourse; they may be triumphs by the orator Anthony—

But, as you know me all, a plain blunt man
That love my friend;

But here I am to speak what I do know;
And I must pause till it come back to me—

or they may be the last words of a dying man:

I kill'd not thee with half so good a will.

They may serve any purpose at the moment. But the purpose they serve at all times is to pour into the ear an unimpeded stream of eloquence, a smooth current of artful sound. And once again it is to be noted that monosyllables are no one speaker's monopoly. The craft is native to them all.

So is the loftier craft of framing superlatives, of condensing infinite compliment into a finite phrase. Antony, being the best orator, does best at this:

With the most noble blood of all this world (III, i, 156)

The choice and master spirits of this age (III, i, 163)

Thou art the ruins of the noblest man
That ever lived in the tide of times (III, i, 256–57)

This was the noblest Roman of them all. (V, v, 68)

But the second best of Brutus is impressive:

That struck the foremost man of all this world (IV, iii, 22)

The last of all the Romans, fare thee well!
It is impossible that ever Rome
Should breed thy fellow. (V, iii, 99–101)

And again the gift is common to the cast.

Their voices are not differentiated then. Nor are their states of mind. Brutus anticipates Hamlet, Othello, Lear, and Macbeth when he soliloquizes concerning the disorder in his soul:

> Between the acting of a dreadful thing
> And the first motion, all the interim is
> Like a phantasma or a hideous dream.
> The Genius and the mortal instruments
> Are then in council; and the state of a man,
> Like to a little kingdom, suffers then
> The nature of an insurrection. (II, i, 63–69)

This is fine, like everything else in *Julius Caesar,* but it is rotund and political, and it was relatively easy for Brutus to say; nor is it impossible to imagine another man's saying it. It is not, like comparable speeches in the tragedies ahead, cut to the individual, and cut with so keen a knife that the individual is dissected in the process and seems to bleed his words. Brutus addresses us through a wrapping of rhetoric, of public speech. And this wrapping is around the imageries of blood and sleep which are so prominent in the play—so prominent, and yet, if one remembers *Macbeth,* so remote from contact with us. The blood that smears the entire surface of *Macbeth* is physical; we see, feel, and smell it. Not so with Caesar's blood; it is "noble" and "costly" because Caesar was the foremost man of all the world, but it remains a metaphor, a political metaphor, distant from the experience of our senses. It may be significant that it can pour from Caesar's statue as well as from his body (II, ii, 76–79), and that when he falls at the base of Pompey's statue it too runs red. There is as much real blood in *Julius Caesar* as there is in stone. And Brutus, once more ancestor to Macbeth, cannot sleep. At home before the assassination, in his tent on the eve of battle, and facing death in his last hour, his lids are heavy, his bones want rest. Yet the fact is not ghastly as in the case of one who will murder Sleep itself, and whose resulting exhaustion will visit itself upon the audience. The fatigue of Brutus is the noble tiredness of a great man, and we respect it; but our pity for the sufferer is not tinged with fear. This is the noblest Roman of them all, and even in distress he keeps his distance.

In such an atmosphere Caesar has little chance to be himself, yet Shakespeare has permitted him to make the most of it. Caesar is not a noble Roman, not one of Plutarch's men. He is that rarity in the play, an Elizabethan personality; he is one of Shakespeare's men. While he lasts he reveals himself in his irregularity, not in his symmetry, in picturesqueness rather than in pose. His monosyllables—for he speaks them too—tell us that he is deficient in one of the senses:

> Come on my right hand, for this ear is deaf; (I, ii, 213)

that he changes his mind suddenly, with no reason given:

> He is a dreamer; let us leave him. Pass; (I, ii, 24)
>
> The cause is in my will; I will not come; (II, ii, 71)

and that he is inordinately vain:

> But there's but one in all doth hold his place.
> So in the world; . . . and that I am he. (III, i, 65–70)

His enemies tell us that he has the falling sickness (I, ii, 256), that he is gullible to flattery (II, i, 207–8), that he is superstitious grown of late and loves to be regaled with wondrous tales of unicorns, bears, lions, and elephants (II, i, 195–206). He appears, indeed, only in his singularity; and he appears but briefly before he falls at the hands of men so completely unlike him that the difference alone might pass as motive for their hatred. Their hatred is of a man not noble, a man who has not suppressed himself. And for a similar reason they distrust Antony, who revels long o' nights (II, ii, 116) and whose orator's tongue flicks unfairly with the serpent speed of irony. They cannot cope with his irony; it is a thing to which solemn men feel superior, and so, since they are not only solemn but innocent, it is a thrust they cannot parry. It is what destroys them, along with much mischance and the heaped mountain of their blunders. They never know him as we do; they do not hear him, for example, prick down the character of Lepidus with epigrams as merciless as bullets (IV, i). They never know the force that is coiled behind his charm. Nor do we know it as we shall in *Antony and Cleopatra*. But it is here, if only briefly as in the case of the eccentric Caesar.

The blunders of Brutus and Cassius, but particularly of Brutus, are many and pathetic. If they do not achieve the dignity of tragic error, of heroic fault, the trouble is with the men who make them; their virtues are not positive enough. This is less true of Cassius, who misconstrues everything at Philippi and so brings on the catastrophe (V, iii, 84). Throughout the play he has been the sharper figure. Caesar defines him in negative terms—"he hears no music" and "loves no plays" as Antony does, and "seldom he smiles" (I, ii, 203–5)—and yet it is from the same source that we learn something we never forget: "a lean and hungry look . . . such men are dangerous." His voice is lean and hungry too, as his mind is rank and practical; when Brutus sees Antony after the assassination he thinks of nothing but assuring him of his "kind love, good thoughts, and reverence," whereas Cassius is only waiting till he can ask:

> But what compact mean you to have with us? (III, i, 215)

Brutus has no patience with the poet who sneaks in at Philippi:

> What should the wars do with these jigging fools?

But Cassius rasps out an angrier rebuke:

> Ha, ha! how vilely doth this cynic rhyme! (IV, iii, 133)

He is the angrier of the two when they quarrel, and therefore he is dramatically the more interesting. He has more flaws than Brutus, who indeed has none except the dramatic one of an impenetrable and inexpressible nobility.

The mistakes of Brutus are the mistakes of a man whose nobility muffles his intelligence. His conquest of himself has extended to his wit; his excellence is not inconsistent with a certain lethargy of mind. He knows this well enough:

> I am not gamesome; I do lack some part
> Of that quick spirit that is in Antony. (I, ii, 28–29)

His honesty is absolute and disarming, so that he will not wait as Cassius does for Caesar to compare him unfavorably with the one brilliant person of the play. But honesty in him is humorless and edgeless; it rings a little dully in our ears, and even a little smugly:

> There is no terror, Cassius, in your threats,
> For I am arm'd so strong in honesty
> That they pass by me as the idle wind,
> Which I respect not. (IV, iii, 66–69)

He would not call this boasting; he would call it the truth, as indeed it is; but the fact that it is, and that he is the speaker, tells us everything about him. Neither would he admit that his behavior to Messala when Messala brings him the news of Portia's death is a piece of acting.

> *Brutus.* Now, as you are a Roman, tell me true.
> *Messala.* Then like a Roman bear the truth I tell:
> For certain she is dead, and by strange manner.

> *Brutus.* Why, farewell, Portia. We must die, Messala.
> With meditating that she must die once,
> I have the patience to endure it now.
> *Messala.* Even so great men great losses should endure.
> *Cassius.* I have as much of this in art as you,
> But yet my nature could not bear it so.
> *Brutus.* Well, to our work alive. What do you think
> Of marching to Philippi presently?
> (IV, iii, 187–97)

He would call it a demonstration of how Stoic gentlemen should conduct themselves. And in truth it is. Brutus already knows of Portia's death, for we have heard him telling Cassius of it. Cassius then is assisting him in the act, and Messala is being impressed as he should be. It is not vanity. It is virtue, it is true manhood demonstrating itself for the benefit of others. But to say as much is again to say that Brutus is humorlessly good. If his duty is to know himself, his performance fails. Nobility has numbed him until he cannot see himself for his principles. When his principles are expressing themselves they are beautiful in their clarity; his consideration for the tired boy Lucius is exquisite (IV, iii), and his last compliment to mankind should have been deserved:

> My heart doth joy that yet in all my life
> I found no man but he was true to me. (V, v, 34–35)

But when he speaks to himself he knows not who is there; he addresses a strange audience, and fumbles. The reasoning with which he convinces himself that Caesar should be murdered is woefully inadequate.

> So Caesar may;
> Then, lest he may, prevent. (II, i, 27–28)

The soliloquy of which these pitiful phrases are a part is riddled with rank fallacy. The fine man is a coarse thinker, the saint of self-denial has little self left to deny.

Shakespeare has done all that could be done with such a man, but what could be done was limited. The hero is heavy in the poet's hands; his reticence prevents intimacy, so that his blunders—as a conspirator with respect to Antony and as a general with respect to the time for attack—are difficult to excuse, they do not arouse in us any instinct to insist that to fail as such a man fails is to be glorious after all. Even the gentleness which will not let him desire Antony's death is in the last analysis confused. He is not mad, or haunted, or inspired, or perplexed in the extreme. He is simply confused. And the grounds of confusion in a man so negative are not to be known. Neither perhaps are they to be known in a man like Hamlet who uncovers something in himself with every word he utters. Yet we know the man—so well that his very attempts to evade us bring him closer. Hamlet may seldom mean what he says; and Shakespeare will never commit the error of exposing him in thought as he exposes Brutus; but we shall be instantly aware of what he means, at any rate to us, and we shall not fail to measure the disturbance in a too much changed mind.

Decius

by John Palmer

There is no reason to believe that Shakespeare had any great respect for men in public life. The evidence is all the other way:

> Get thee glass eyes,
> And, like a scurvy politician, seem
> To see the things thou dost not.

But the Elizabethans expected to find upon the stage kings, princes, and generals. The dramatist must therefore fill his scene with political figures. His audience must behold these great ones sitting in council, leading their men into battle, climbing to power or declining to impotence. Shakespeare, taking from Holinshed or Plutarch a story or situation which enabled him to fulfill these expectations, found himself willy-nilly writing a political play. But his characters interested him first and foremost as men; it is an accident that they should be men prominent in public affairs or hoping to be so. It is, indeed, a strange paradox that Shakespeare who, above all other dramatists, was preoccupied with the private mind and heart of the individual, should have written a group of plays unmatched in any literature for their political content.

Shakespeare, since he is forced to take the political field, broadens it to include all human activities in which private passion or personal conviction is brought into relation with public life. For Shakespeare there arises a political issue in the larger sense whenever an individual is required to adjust himself to the practical necessities of his position in a kingdom or commonwealth, to shape a policy or control its application. Brutus, the republican philosopher, is asked to accept the absolute rule of Caesar; Richard II, wayward and introspective, is compelled to measure his frail genius against the cold efficiency of Bolingbroke; Henry V is summoned to show posterity a successful man

---

"Decius." From Political Characters of Shakespeare *by John Palmer (London: Macmillan & Co., Ltd., 1945), pp. vi–vii, 40–43. Reprinted by permission of St. Martin's Press, Inc.*

of action conforming instinctively with the genius of his countrymen and emerging triumphantly as master of the event; Richard III is called upon to exhibit an unbridled intelligence in the attainment and exercise of power; Coriolanus presents the aristocrat in a vain effort to come to terms with the common man. Grouped around these principal figures of the political scene is a crowd of courtiers, prelates and councillors; of loyalists and rebels; of zealous partisans or detached observers; of men who follow their principles or seize their opportunities. Almost every kind of man to be met with in public life, great or mean, wise or foolish, wicked or virtuous, simple or subtle, calculating or generous, is to be found in these plays. Some are sketched with a few apparently negligent strokes; others are drawn with elaborate care. All can be recognised as political characters who have their counterparts in every generation. . . .

Decius, in his colloquy with Caesar, presents an attitude typical of the public servant who is accustomed to deal with persons in high office. He knows Caesar to be great, but refuses to be impressed. He is the junior minister or high official who seeks compensation for accepting the supremacy of an abler man by indulging a humorous perspicacity at his expense and airing an intimate acquaintance with his foibles. He is the courtier, inwardly proud of his access to august circles, who nevertheless affects a smiling disparagement of the privilege. He is the man who lives for a ribbon, but professes amusement at having to wear it. He will inform you that His Excellency is peevish this morning, having eaten or drunk unwisely the night before; that His Worship grows every day more difficult to manage and is every day more easily misled. He is the man to whom the absurdities of public life are very tolerable, provided they can be successfully exploited and at the same time afford him opportunities for the exercise of a small wit at the expense of a great man. He is the universal valet to whom no one is ever a hero. He sounds an echo, through the ages, of pleasantry exchanged in antechambers, lobbies, corridors or other purlieus where little people attend their masters. He is that familiar creature of the alcove who is always ready to claim that he can drop the right word into the right ear at the right moment.

It was Cassius, discussing ways and means with Brutus in his orchard, who first raised the question: What if Caesar should decide not to attend the meeting of the senate?

> For he is superstitious grown of late,
> Quite from the main opinion he held once

Of fantasy, of dreams, and ceremonies:
It may be, these apparent prodigies,
The unaccustom'd terror of this night,
And the persuasion of his augurers,
May hold him from the Capitol to-day.

Decius jumps at the occasion. This is just his line of country:

Never fear that: if he be so resolved,
I can o'ersway him; for he loves to hear
That unicorns may be betray'd with trees,
And bears with glasses, elephants with holes,
Lions with toils, and men with flatterers;

Let me work;
For I can give his humour the true bent,
And I will bring him to the Capitol.

He catches Caesar in one of his majestic attitudes:

Decius. Caesar, all hail! good morrow, worthy Caesar:
I come to fetch you to the senate-house.
Caesar. And you are come in very happy time,
To bear my greeting to the senators,
And tell them that I will not come to-day:
Cannot, is false, and that I dare not, falser:
I will not come to-day: tell them so, Decius.
Calpurnia. Say he is sick.
Caesar. Shall Caesar send a lie?
Have I in conquest stretch'd mine arm so far,
To be afeard to tell greybeards the truth?
Decius, go tell them Caesar will not come.

Decius is outwardly respectful but inwardly amused. With deference he suggests that Caesar's message may be found ridiculous:

Most mighty Caesar, let me know some cause,
Lest I be laugh'd at when I tell them so.

Caesar condescends to explain. Calpurnia has dreamed that his statue spouted blood and that many lusty Romans came smiling and bathed their hands in it. Decius, not in the least deceived by Caesar's pretence that he is staying at home to please his wife, sets out to show that the dream is not a bad but a good omen:

This dream is all amiss interpreted;
It was a vision fair and fortunate:
Your statue spouting blood in many pipes,

In which so many smiling Romans bathed,
Signifies that from you great Rome shall suck
Reviving blood, and that great men shall press
For tinctures, stains, relics, and cognizance.
This by Calpurnia's dream is signified.

Caesar accepts this interpretation and Decius presses his advantage. He speaks now to the small Caesar whom he claims to know so well. He can address this Caesar in a spirit of mockery which he hardly troubles to conceal—promise him a bauble, declare openly that people may laugh at him or throw doubt upon his courage:

The senate have concluded
To give this day a crown to mighty Caesar.
If you shall send them word you will not come,
Their minds may change. Besides, it were a mock
Apt to be render'd, for some one to say
"Break up the senate till another time,
When Caesar's wife shall meet with better dreams."
If Caesar hide himself, shall not they whisper
"Lo, Caesar is afraid"?

Decius has successfully performed his mission and Caesar makes ready to accompany him. At this moment Brutus enters with the conspirators. The short passage in which Caesar greets them brings him suddenly to life again. He has a word for everyone and it is the right word. This is the real Caesar, courteous and accessible, who has it in him to win hearts and to command respect:

Caius Ligarius,
Caesar was ne'er so much your enemy
As that same ague which has made you lean.

See! Antony, that revels long o'nights,
Is notwithstanding up. Good morrow, Antony.

Bid them prepare within:
I am to blame to be thus waited for.
Now, Cinna; now, Metellus; what, Trebonius!
I have an hour's talk in store for you;
Remember that you call on me to-day:
Be near me, that I may remember you.

The scene concludes with Caesar's invitation to take wine with him. Henceforth Caesar, the man, is lost in Caesar's effigy.

Antony

by Harley Granville-Barker

There is a tide in the affairs of men
Which, taken at the flood, leads on to fortune. . . .

Mark Antony cannot always talk so wisely, but he takes the tide that Brutus loses. He is a born opportunist, and we see him best in the light of his great opportunity. He stands contrasted with both Cassius and Brutus, with the man whom his fellows respect the more for his aloofness, and with such a rasping colleague as Cassius must be. Antony is, above all things, a good sort.

Shakespeare keeps him in ambush throughout the first part of the play. Up to the time when he faces the triumphant conspirators he speaks just thirty-three words. But there have already been no less than seven separate references to him, all significant. And this careful preparation culminates as significantly in the pregnant message he sends by his servant from the house to which it seems he has fled, bewildered by the catastrophe of Cæsar's death. Yet, as we listen, it is not the message of a very bewildered man. Antony, so far, is certainly —in what we might fancy would be his own lingo—a dark horse. And, though we may father him on Plutarch, to English eyes there can be no more typically English figure than the sportsman turned statesman, but a sportsman still. Such men range up and down our history. Antony is something besides, however, that we used to flatter ourselves was not quite so English. He can be, when occasion serves, the perfect demagogue. Nor has Shakespeare any illusions as to what the harsher needs of politics may convert your sportsman once he is out to kill. The conspirators are fair game doubtless. But Lepidus, a little later, will be the carted stag.

"Antony." From Prefaces to Shakespeare: King Lear, Cymbeline, Julius Caesar *by Harley Granville-Barker (London: B. T. Batsford Ltd.; Princeton, N. J.: Princeton University Press, 1965), II, 175–81.*

A barren-spirited fellow; one that feeds
On abject orts and imitations,
Which, out of use and staled by other men,
Begin his fashion: do not talk of him
But as a property . . .

to serve the jovial Antony's turn! This is your good sort, your sportsman, your popular orator, stripped very bare.

The servant's entrance with Antony's message, checking the conspirators' triumph, significant in its insignificance, is the turning point of the play.[1] But Shakespeare plucks further advantage from it. It allows him to bring Antony out of ambush completely effective and in double guise; the message foreshadows him as politician, a minute later we see him grieving deeply for his friend's death. There is, of course, nothing incompatible in the two aspects of the man, but the double impression is all-important. He must impress us as uncalculatingly abandoned to his feelings, risking his very life to vent them. For a part of his strength lies in impulse; he can abandon himself to his feelings, as Brutus the philosopher cannot. Moreover, this bold simplicity is his safe-conduct now. Were the conspirators not impressed by it, did it not seem to obliterate his politic side, they might well and wisely take him at his word and finish with him then and there. And at the back of his mind Antony has this registered clearly enough. It must be with something of the sportsman's—and the artist's—happy recklessness that he flings the temptation at them:

Live a thousand years,
I shall not find myself so apt to die:
No place will please me so, no mean of death,
As here by Cæsar, and by you cut off,
The choice and master spirits of this age.

He means it; but he knows, as he says it, that there is no better way of turning the sword of a so flattered choice and master spirit aside. It is this politic, shadowed aspect of Antony that is to be their undoing; so Shakespeare is concerned to keep it clear at the back of our minds too. Therefore he impresses it on us first by the servant's speech, and Antony himself is free a little later to win us and the conspirators both.

Not that the politician does not begin to peep pretty soon. He tactfully ignores the cynicism of Cassius,

[1] As Moulton demonstrates in an admirable passage.

> Your voice shall be as strong as any man's
> In the disposing of new dignities.

But by Brutus' reiterated protest that Cæsar was killed in wise kindness what realist, what ironist—and Antony is both—would not be tempted?

> I doubt not of your wisdom.
> Let each man render me his bloody hand. . . .

And, in bitter irony, he caps their ritual with his own. It is the ritual of friendship, but of such a friendship as the blood of Cæsar, murdered by his friends, may best cement. To Brutus the place of honor in the compact; to each red-handed devotee his due; and last, but by no means least, in Antony's love shall be Trebonius who drew him away while the deed was done. And so to the final, most fitting apostrophe:

> Gentlemen all!

Emotion subsided, the politician plays a good game. They shall never be able to say he approved their deed; but he is waiting, please, for those convincing reasons that Cæsar was dangerous. He even lets slip a friendly warning to Cassius that the prospect is not quite clear. Then, with yet more disarming frankness, comes the challenging request to Brutus to let him speak in the market place. As he makes it, a well-calculated request! For how can Brutus refuse, how admit a doubt that the Roman people will not approve this hard service done them? Still, that there may be no doubt at all, Brutus will first explain everything to his fellow-citizens himself, lucidly and calmly. When reason has made sure of her sway, the emotional, the "gamesome," Antony may do homage to his friend.

> Be it so;
> I do desire no more.

responds Antony, all docility and humility, all gravity—though if ever a smile could sharpen words, it could give a grim edge to these. So they leave him with dead Cæsar.

In this contest thus opened between the man of high argument and the instinctive politician, between principle (mistaken or not) and opportunism, we must remember that Antony can be by no means confident of success. He foresees chaos. He knows, if these bemused patriots do not, that it takes more than correct republican doctrines to replace a great man. But as to this Roman mob—this citizenry, save the mark!—whoever knows which way it will turn? The odds are on the whole against him. Still he'll try his luck; Octavius, though, had better keep safely out of the way meanwhile. All his senses are sharpened by emergency. Before ever Octavius' servant can speak he has recognized the fellow and guessed the errand. Shakespeare shows us his mind at its swift work, its purposes shaping.

> Passion, I see, is catching, for mine eyes,
> Seeing those beads of sorrow stand in thine,
> Began to water.

—from which it follows that if the sight of Cæsar's body can so move the man and the man's tears so move him, why, his own passion may move his hearers in the market place presently to some purpose! His imagination, once it takes fire, flashes its way along, not by reason's slow process though in reason's terms.[2]

To what he is to move his hearers we know: and it will be worth while later to analyze the famous speech, that triumph of histrionics. For though the actor of Antony must move us with it also—and he can scarcely fail to—Shakespeare has set him the further, harder and far more important task of showing us an Antony the mob never see, of making him clear to us, moreover, even while we are stirred by his eloquence, of making clear to us just by what it is we are stirred. It would, after all, be pretty poor playwriting and acting which could achieve no more than a plain piece of mob oratory, however gorgeous; a pretty poor compliment to an audience to ask of it no subtler response than the mob's. But to show us, and never for a moment to

[2] How many modern actors upon their picture stage, with its curtain to close a scene for them pat upon some triumphant top note, have brought this one to its end twenty lines earlier upon the familiar, tremendous, breathless apostrophe (did Shakespeare ever pen such another sentence?) that begins,

> Woe to the hand that shed this costly blood!
> Over thy wounds now do I prophesy . . .

But to how untimely an end! The mechanism of Shakespeare's theater forbade such effects. Cæsar's body is lying on the main stage, and must be removed, and it will take at least two people to carry it. Here is one reason for the arrival of Octavius' servant. But as ever with Shakespeare, and with any artist worth his salt, limitation is turned to advantage. If dead Cæsar is to be the mainspring of the play's further action, what more forceful way could be found of making this plain than, for a finish to the scene, to state the new theme of Octavius' coming, Cæsar's kin and successor?

let slip from our sight, the complete and complex Antony, impulsive and calculating, warm-hearted and callous, aristocrat, sportsman and demagogue, that will be for the actor an achievement indeed; and the playwright has given him all the material for it.

Shakespeare himself knows, no one better, what mere histrionics may amount to. He has been accused of showing in a later play (but unjustly, I hold) his too great contempt for the mob; he might then have felt something deeper than contempt for the man who could move the mob by such means; he may even have thought Brutus made the better speech. Antony, to be sure, is more than an actor; for one thing he writes his own part as he goes along. But he gathers the ideas for it as he goes too, with no greater care for their worth than the actor need have so long as they are effective at the moment. He lives abundantly in the present, his response to its call is unerring. He risks the future. How does the great oration end?

> Mischief, thou are afoot;
> Take thou what course thou wilt!

A wicked child, one would say, that has whipped up his fellow-children to a riot of folly and violence. That is one side of him. But the moment after he is off, brisk, cool and businesslike, to play the next move in the game with that very cool customer, Octavius.

He has had no tiresome principles to consult or to expound.

> I only speak right on. . . .

he boasts;

> I tell you that which you yourselves do know. . . .

An admirable maxim for popular orators and popular writers too! There is nothing aloof, nothing superior about Antony. He may show a savage contempt for this man or that; he has a sort of liking for men in the mass. He is, in fact, the common man made perfect in his commonness; yet he is perceptive of himself as of his fellows, and, even so, content.

What follows upon his eloquent mourning for Cæsar? When the chaos in Rome has subsided he ropes his "merry fortune" into harness. It is not a very pleasant colloquy with which the fourth act opens.

> *Antony.* These many then shall die; their names are pricked.
> *Octavius.* Your brother too must die; consent you, Lepidus?
> *Lepidus.* I do consent.

Octavius. Prick him down, Antony.
Lepidus. Upon condition Publius shall not live,
Who is your sister's son, Mark Antony.
Antony. He shall not live; look, with a spot I damn him.

The conspirators have, of course, little right to complain. But four lines later we learn that Lepidus himself, when his two friends have had their use of him, is to fare not much better than his brother—than the brother he has himself just given so callously to death! Can he complain either, then? This is the sort of beneficence the benevolent Brutus has let loose on the world.

But Antony finishes the play in fine form; victorious in battle, politically magnanimous to a prisoner or two, and ready with a resounding tribute to Brutus, now that he lies dead. Not in quite such fine form, though; for the shadow of that most unsportsmanlike young man Octavius is already moving visibly to his eclipse.

These, then are the three men among whom Shakespeare divides this dramatic realm; the idealist, the egoist, the opportunist. The contrast between them must be kept clear in the acting by all that the actors do and are, for upon its tension the living structure of the play depends. And, it goes without saying, they must be shown to us as fellow-creatures, not as abstractions from a dead past. For so Shakespeare saw them; and, if he missed something of the mind of the Roman, yet these three stand with sufficient truth for the sum of the human forces, which in any age, and in ours as in his, hold the world in dispute.

Shakespeare's Stage Blood and Its Critical Significance

by Leo Kirschbaum

The Elizabethans were familiar with scenes in which stage blood was liberally used. The tradition was old. In *Cambises* (1560's), "Enter Cruelty and Murder with bloody hands." They grasp their victim:

> [*Cru.*] Even now I strike, his body to wound.
> *Strike him in divers places.*
> Beholde, now his blood springs out on the ground!
> *A little bladder of vinegar prickt.*

Spectacular blood effects were created by painting, smearing, or sprinkling and by concealed bladders, sponges, and animal entrails. In *Locrine,* King Humber appears after the battle with "his armes all bloodie." In *Titus Andronicus,* Tamora's sons are bound. "Enter Titus Andronicus with a knife, and Lauinia with a Bason." Then, "He cuts their throats" on-stage. Nashe was probably referring to IV. vii of *I Henry VI* when he wrote of the spectators "who in the Tragedian that represents his [Talbot's] person, imagine they behold him fresh bleeding." The initial direction of Marston's *Antonio's Revenge* is "Enter *Piero,* unbrac't, his armes bare, smeer'd in blood, a poniard in one hand bloodie." In the same dramatist's *Sophonisba* "Enter *Massinissa* . . . his arme transfixt with a dart." Jugurth cries, "Uncle your blood flows fast, pray ye withdraw." Asdrubal also comments on Massinissa's "waste of blood." Eighty lines after the above entrance, Jugurth plucks the weapon out of his uncle's wound. In Chapman's *Caesar and Pompey,* Crassineus enters, "a sword, as thrust through his face; he fals." In the same play, Cato falls on his sword on-stage. Cleanthes says, "He hath ript his entrals." When Cleanthes offers to

---

"Shakespeare's Stage Blood and Its Critical Significance" by Leo Kirschbaum. From PMLA, *LXIV (1949), 517–24. Reprinted by permission of the Modern Language Association.*

"sew them vp Being yet vnperisht," Cato replies, "Stand off; now they are not," and the stage direction reads, *"He thrusts him back and plucks out his entrals."* In Beaumont and Fletcher's *The Maid's Tragedy,* after the on-stage stabbing of the king, "Enter Evadne, her arms bloody, with a knife." In Jonson's *Catiline,* the conspirators have their individual goblets filled from a bowl of mixed wine and blood. In *Appius and Virginia,* "Enter Virginius with his knife, that and his arms stript up to the elbowes all bloudy." Comments G. F. Reynolds, "So this trail of blood runs through the whole period and beyond. It must have been a messy nuisance; but what of that, we may hear the stage manager saying, if he could give the 'understanding gentleman' a deeper thrill." [1]

But what of Shakespeare and his gore-spattered dramatis personae? The scholars have little to say. Creizenach writes, "In the same way, at the beginning of *Macbeth,* the wounded sergeant is required to enter 'bleeding,' and the text itself leaves no doubt that Macbeth came in after the murder with blood-stained hands." He also refers to *Titus Andronicus.* Lawrence writes, "But there is no need to pillory Marston, when effects of this order are to be found in Shakespeare and Webster. Read the first act of *Coriolanus,* and note how, after Marcius has entered bleeding, Cominius refers to him as looking like a flayed man; note also how Marcius speaks later of 'this painting/Wherein you see me smear'd.' "

The editors of *A Companion to Shakespeare Studies* (1934) declare in their Preface, "The student's approach to Shakespeare, as the work of the last thirty years has planned it, will be something like a *contemporary* approach. He will try to make himself one with the audience at the Globe or Blackfriars." But of the tangible, sensory actuality of the Elizabethan stage, there is little in the *Companion.* Although we today are fond of insisting that a Shakespeare play must be looked at as a play, as an Elizabethan play, as a dramatic poem, above all as a totality, I am not so sure that we always *do* want to see a Shakespeare play as Shakespeare planned it for the stage. We seem anxious not to have the Bard confused with those other Grand Guignol experts: Kyd, Chapman, Marston, Tourneur, Webster, Ford, *et al.* At opposite ex-

[1] *The Staging of Elizabethan Plays At the Red Bull Theater 1605–1625* (New York: MLA, 1940), p. 41. My sources for the above paragraph have largely been Reynolds, pp. 40–41, 85; Wilhelm Creizenach, *The English Drama in the Age of Shakespeare* (Philadelphia-London, 1916), p. 403; W. J. Lawrence, *Pre-Restoration Stage Studies* (Harvard Univ. Press, 1927), pp. 235–41. All the items selected from these three have been examined in and taken from the original texts themselves.

tremes, neither the careful student of poetic texture, like L. C. Knights, nor the subtle student of production problems, like Harley Granville-Barker, seems to care to deal with the many severed heads, tortures, murders, duels, blood baths that are scattered through the First Folio's pages. Even in L. L. Schücking's British Academy Lecture (1938), "The Baroque Character of the Elizabethan Tragic Hero," in which Shakespeare's Othello, Macbeth, Lear, and Hamlet are described as containing the spectacular characteristics of the general category of Elizabethan protagonists (although it is pointed out that Shakespeare, unlike his contemporaries, "naturalized" his heroes), there seems to be a reluctance on Schücking's part to attach the Shakespeare hero's spectacular character to the spectacular properties and scenes of the play.

Therefore in the present paper, I would like to dwell fully on two spectacular blood effects that Shakespeare employed and to try to show that these effects are extremely important for the full aesthetic richness of the plays concerned—as important as poetry, character, and plot. In a word, I wish to make this paper an experiment in trusting Shakespeare.

Let us first look at *Julius Caesar*. In order to show how unprepared present-day sensibility is for blood scenes in Shakespeare, let me quote from a well-known modern critic:

> Brutus addresses us through a wrapping of rhetoric, of public speech. And this wrapping is around the imageries of blood and sleep which are so prominent in the play—so prominent, and yet, if one remembers *Macbeth*, so remote from contact with us. The blood that smears the entire surface of *Macbeth* is physical; we see, feel, and smell it. Not so with Caesar's blood; it is 'noble' and 'costly' because Caesar was the foremost man of all the world, but it remains a metaphor, a political metaphor, distant from the experience of our senses. It may be significant that it can pour from Caesar's statue as well as from his body (II, ii, 76–79), and that when he falls at the base of Pompey's statue it too runs red. There is as much real blood in *Julius Caesar* as there is in stone.[2]

Examine, however, the scene of Caesar's murder, Calpurnia had dreamt, says Caesar,

> she saw my statue
> Which like a Fountaine, with an hundred spouts
> Did run pure blood: and many lusty Romans
> Came smiling, & did bathe their hands in it:

[2] Mark Van Doren, *Shakespeare* (New York, 1939), p. 185.

This dream becomes an actuality. Immediately after the tyrannicide, the conspirators are highly excited. Suddenly Brutus bends to the bleeding corpse.

Stoope Romans, stoope,
And let vs bathe our hands in *Caesars* blood
Vp to the Elbowes, and besmeare our Swords:
Then walke we forth, euen to the Market place,
And wauing our red Weapons o're our heads,
Let's all cry Peace, Freedome, and Liberty.
Cassi. Stoop then, and wash. How many Ages hence
Shall this our lofty Scene be acted ouer,
In State vnborne, and Accents yet vnknowne?
Bru. How many times shall *Caesar* bleed in sport,
That now on *Pompeyes* Basis lye[s] along,
No worthier then the dust?
Cassi. So oft as that shall be,
So often shall the knot of vs be call'd,
The Men that gaue their Country liberty.
Dec. What, shall we forth?
Cassi. I, euery man away.
Brutus shall leade, and we will grace his heeles
With the most boldest, and best hearts of Rome.
Enter a Seruant.

That the indicated actions were indeed done and exploited full-view of the audience is indicated by succeeding references. Antony speaks of

your Swords; made rich
With the most Noble blood of all this World.
I do beseech yee, if you beare me hard,
Now, whil'st your purpled hands do reeke and smoake,
Fulfill your pleasure.

Brutus says to him:

Though now we must appeare bloody and cruell,
As by our hands, and this our present Acte
You see we do: Yet see you but our hands,
And this, the bleeding businesse they haue done:

Antony stretches out his hand to each of the death-dealers:

Let each man render me his bloody hand.
First *Marcus Brutus* will I shake with you;
Next *Caius Cassius* do I take your hand;

Now *Decius Brutus* yours; now yours *Metellus;*
Yours *Cinna;* and my valiant *Caska,* yours;
Though last, not least in loue, yours good *Trebonius.* . . .
That I did loue thee *Caesar,* O 'tis true:
If then thy Spirit looke vpon vs now,
Shall it not greeue thee deerer then thy death,
To see thy *Antony* making his peace,
Shaking the bloody fingers of thy Foes?

The bathing of the hands in Caesar's bloody corpse and the smearing of the swords are, then, not metaphorical at all. They are naturalistic stage effects *coram populo* deliberately meant by Shakespeare for actual production and undoubtedly achieved at the Globe. It is interesting to inquire what past and present critics and producers have done with Shakespeare's intentions here.

In his text, Pope assigned the "Stoope Romans, stoope," speech to Casca and wrote: "In all the editions this speech is ascribed to Brutus, than which nothing is more inconsistent with his mild and philosophical character." Theobald thought Pope "more nice than wise" in this change:

> Brutus esteemed the death of Caesar a sacrifice to liberty; and as such gloried in his heading the enterprize. Besides, our author is strictly copying history. "Brutus and his followers, being yet hot with the murder, marched in a body from the Senate-house to the Capitol with their drawn swords, with an air of confidence and assurance."—Plutarch, *Caesar,* #45. And: "Brutus and his party betook themselves to the Capitol, and in their way shewing their hands all bloody, and their naked swords, proclaiming liberty to the people."—Ibid., *Brutus,* #13.

Upton (1746) wrote:

> This was agreeable to an ancient and religious custom. So in Æschylus we read that the seven captains, who came against Thebes, sacrificed a bull, and dipped their hands in the gore, invoking at the same time the gods of war, and binding themselves with an oath to revenge the cause of Eteocles (*Seven Against Thebes,* v, 42) . . . By this solemn action Brutus gives the assassination of Caesar a religious air and turn.

Capell, too, thought the action "solemn."

> For the action which is ushered in by these words we have seen a preparative [in that passage] where the same speaker opposes shedding any more blood but only Caesar's, which, in his idea, was an offering to the goddess he worshipped most—public liberty; and from this idea results

the action proposed by him; such action having many examples in ancient sacrifices, the more solemn particularly, as this is thought, by the speaker.

In the nineteenth century Knight made some shrewd comments:

> We have seen the stoic Brutus . . . gradually warm up to the great enterprise of asserting his principles by one terrible blow, for triumph or for extinction. The blow is given. The excitement which succeeds is wondrously painted by the poet, without a hint from the historian. The calm of the gentle Brutus is lifted up, for the moment, into an attitude of terrible sublimity. It is he who says: "Stoop, Romans, stoop. . . . Let's all cry, Peace, Freedom, and Liberty!" From that moment the character flags; the calmness returns; something also of the irresolution comes back. Brutus is too high-minded for his position.[3]

In his essay on *Julius Caesar* Granville-Barker, surprisingly, seems to evade the problem of the blood-bath as stage effect:

> We have the helter skelter of the moment after Caesar's fall; Brutus is the only figure of authority and calm. . . . Let them sign themselves ritual brothers—and in whose blood but Caesar's? . . . We need not doubt Brutus' deep sincerity for a moment. . . . And he anoints himself devotedly. Then Cassius, febrile, infatuate: Stoop, then, and wash. . . .[4]

How the audience is to get the notion of a solemn religious sacrifice from the shocking gory effect is not explained by the above critics.[5] The silence of most editors and critics, the pious explanations of

[3] These quotations are from H. H. Furness, Jr., ed., *Julius Caesar,* New Variorum Edition (Philadelphia-London, 1913), pp. 145–46.

[4] *Prefaces to Shakespeare* (Princeton Univ. Press, 1946–47), II, 389–90. I like neither Granville-Barker's juggling of the order of the speeches nor his highly subjective interpretation. Why he believes Brutus comes off well in this scene and Casca and Cassius do not is not made clear. *Cf.* "Our sympathy with Brutus has next to weather the murder, through the planning and doing of which he stalks so nobly and disinterestedly and with such admirable self-control" (p. 355) and "Butchered by Casca, sacrificed by Brutus—these two doings of the same deed are marked and kept apart —Caesar lies dead" (p. 388). But for another play Granville-Barker *can* see the functional significance of a horror scene: "Shakespeare then deals the dreadful blow to Gloucester. The very violence and horror of this finds its dramatic justification in the need to match in another sort—since he could not hope to match it in spiritual intensity—the catastrophe to Lear" (I, 274).

[5] When critics interpret the blood wash in III. i as awe-inspiring ritual, they must be recalling (as Capell indicates) the passage in II. i in which Brutus advises the conspirators not to kill Antony along with Caesar. But the critics are then contaminating III. I with II. i and confusing intention with act. The least one can say of the blood bath is what John Palmer says (my italics): "Brutus [carries] to *dreadful extremes* the sacrificial mood in which he struck the fatal blow"—*Political Characters of Shakespeare* (London, 1945), p. 14.

others, seem indicative of some kind of turning away from the unseemly. None of them appears willing to face the scene in its own maculate terms.

The critics are in line with the producers. Eighteenth and nineteenth century productions did not contain the lines and action we have been discussing. In *Shakespeare and the Actors, The Stage Business in His Plays (1660–1905)*, A. C. Sprague informs us:

> Brutus bids the conspirators stoop with him and bathe their hands in Caesar's blood. "Stoop then and wash," Cassius replies. But on the stage this was seldom done. What is more the lines themselves were quietly altered, the idea underlying the changes, which vary in different editions, being always that these dignified Romans were *not* to "stoop and wash."
>
> In Bell's edition [1774], lines 111 ff. (including Rowe's direction, "Dipping their swords in *Caesar's* blood") are quoted, as "seldom delivered on the stage." [6]

As Knight recognized, there is no warrant in the source for the blood-bathing action. Nevertheless, North's Plutarch may have suggested it. In the life of Brutus, we read that when the conspirators were stabbing Caesar, "so many swords and daggers lighting upon one body, one of them hurt another, and among them Brutus caught a blow on his hand, because he would make one in murdering of him, and all the rest also were every man of them bloodied." Afterwards, "Brutus and his consorts, having their swords bloody in their hands, went straight to the Capitol, persuading the Romans as they went to take their liberty again." Antony shows the common people "Caesar's gown all bloody." In the life of Caesar, the victim "was hacked and mangled among them, as a wild beast taken of hunters." He was driven "against the base whereupon Pompey's image stood, which ran

[6] (Harvard Univ. Press, 1945), pp. 321, 427. That an earlier stage tradition was faithful to Shakespeare may be indicated by Voltaire's words in 1731 concerning a London production in which he saw Brutus speak to the mob, "tenant encore un poignard teint du sang de César" (quoted *ibid.*, p. 323). "Tree . . . used the business [of blood washing] (Irving's eagerly awaited comment on his production was 'H'm—yes—too much blood!') and, when Antony shakes hands with the conspirators, 'Casca with rude intent and purposeful cruelty smirches with a crimson stain the arm of butchered Caesar's friend' " (pp. 321–22). Percy Simpson tells us a bit more about the Tree production: "Gathering round the body, the conspirators reddened their hands in blood—a graphic touch usually omitted in acting copies, as its significance depends upon a hunting custom long obsolete. . . . As each man 'rendered him [Antony] his bloody hand,' the blunt Casca wiped off the stains on Antony's wrist, and he repressed a rising look of horror" (Furness, *Variorum,* p. 443).

all of a gore-blood till he was slain." "Brutus and his confederates . . . , being yet hot with this murther they had committed, having their swords drawn in their hands, came all in a troop together out of the Senate, and went into the market place . . . boldly holding up their heads like men of courage, and called to the people to defend their liberty. . . ." The plebeians later see Caesar's body "all bemangled with gashes of swords." In the life of Antony, "he unfolded before the whole assembly the bloody garments of the dead, thrust through in many places with their swords, and called the malefactors cruel and cursed murtherers." [7] It has been suggested that Shakespeare's source for the blood-wash may have been a passage in the life of Publicola in which the conspirators plan to seal their pact by sacrificing a man, drinking his blood, and shaking hands in his bowels.[8]

Shakespeare, therefore, invented the blood-bath, deliberately gave the proposal for it to Brutus, and followed it with the invention of the bloody handshaking action with Antony.

What, then, are Shakespeare's intentions? They are, of course, multiple. If proper attention is paid to the above lines and stage effects as integral parts of Shakespeare's design, much revelatory criticism will undoubtedly ensue. I think we can be fairly sure of the five following glosses: (1) Shakespeare introduces a scene which in its novelty and brutality excites the spectators and grasps their attention. (2) He underscores the fact that the conspirators are bloodthirsty men—even if the audience has already allowed that the motives of some of them were initially respectable. All murder is in the act savage and inhuman, Shakespeare is saying. Whether or not killing ever justifies the doctrine of a bad means serving a good end, the merciless rending of a man is an obscene performance. (3) As Pope saw, that Brutus should suggest the blood-bath comes as a shock. And that is exactly Shakespeare's intention. However they may disagree in particulars, all commentators on Shakespeare's play regard Brutus as a man who does not understand himself or others. That the dignified and gentle Brutus should propose the ghastly procedure of the conspirators bathing their hands in the blood of Caesar's body wrenches the mind. It emphasizes the disorder in the man. The major lesson of Shakespeare's history plays is so simple that its tremendous significance may be overlooked.

[7] C. F. Tucker Brooke, ed., *Shakespeare's Plutarch,* Shakespeare Classics (London, 1909), I, 133–37, 101–4; II, 22.

[8] See Furness, *Variorum,* p. 296; North's Plutarch (1579), Shakespeare Head Press (Oxford, 1928), I, 265.

It is this: *History is made by men.* How frightening this premise really becomes when we see the noble Brutus suddenly turn into a savage! (4) The conspirators openly degenerate precisely at that juncture where Antony begins to fashion the ensuing events. As Moulton,[9] seconded by Granville-Barker,[10] points out, the entrance of Antony's servant is the turning point of the play. (5) The blood of Caesar begins to spread. As critics have noted, the implications of his death overshadow the rest of the drama. He is mighty yet. The dreadful blood which we see covering the hands of the conspirators, then touching Antony's hand, then staining the exhibited mantle, then turning the witless plebeians into destroyers—this is the symbol and mark of the blood and destruction which is to flow through the rest of the play, overwhelming the conspirator's plans, accomplishing Antony's promise to Caesar's butchered corpse.

[9] *Shakespeare as a Dramatic Artist* (Oxford, 1906), pp. 197–98.
[10] *Op. cit.*, II, 366, 390.

The Moral Dilemma in Tragedy: Brutus

by Arthur Sewell

Public decisions, nevertheless, may involve men in private moral crises. In the English histories Shakespeare, except in minor characters, as, for example, in the Duke of York in *Richard II,* does not represent his characters in moral doubt. After the event, perhaps, a character may confess the uncertainties that have attended his decisions:

> God knows, my son,
> By what by-paths and indirect crook'd ways
> I met this crown: and I myself know well
> How troublesome it sat upon my head.

But we rarely see purpose in the English histories coming to a head of decision in the will.

The Roman histories were more remote, and perhaps in *Julius Caesar* Shakespeare felt freer in his dealings with character than he did in the English histories. Besides, Plutarch gave him a different lead from the English Chronicles. In the character of Brutus, certainly, he presents the kind of moral crisis which he never treats in the English plays. The nature and significance of this crisis seem to me to have great importance in the study of Shakespeare's methods of characterization.

According to North's rendering of Plutarch, Brutus "framed his manner of life by the rules of vertue and studie of Philosophie," and Shakespeare allows Brutus's contemporaries (and Brutus himself!) to imitate this tribute in the play. It is clear that such a character, whose constant practice it is to refer his conduct to those principles by which he directs it, will be represented with a good deal of direct self-

---

"The Moral Dilemma in Tragedy: Brutus." From Character and Society in Shakespeare *by Arthur Sewell (Oxford: The Clarendon Press, 1951), pp. 53–56. Reprinted by permission of the publisher.*

revelation. It is also clear, however, that if these principles do in fact absolutely direct conduct, if personality is wholly contained within them, if Brutus is no more and no other than "the noblest Roman of them all," the appeal of the play (in so far as his character is concerned) will be on a very obvious, not to say merely didactic, level. If, when Brutus says that he is "arm'd so strong in Honesty," there is no more than that to be said, his address to the world is not at all discovered in the dramatic transformation of personality into speech and behaviour; it is discovered as an abstraction, in the reduction of personality to a set of principles. And Schücking might be held to have reason when he finds "a certain childishness" in *Julius Caesar* which has always made the play suitable for study in schools.

Before we agree with Schücking we should look at the matter a little more closely. Thus Mr. J. I. M. Stewart . . . suggests that the play (and the study of the character of Brutus) has in it "more subtlety than is readily discernible." He applies to Brutus's reiterated claims to unusual honesty a psychological interpretation, and he holds that these claims show Brutus's motives to have been more selfish than he himself suspected. He believes that Brutus, with some intellectual dishonesty, uses a form of self-deception to "cheer himself up." Brutus, Mr. J. I. M. Stewart suggests, keeps insisting to himself that he is honest in order to keep out of his consciousness the wrinkling doubts.

This interpretation, which is little more than a sophisticating application of the maxim *Qui s'excuse s'accuse,* will surely never do. There is another explanation in which not only Shakespeare's subtlety but also an important, perhaps the most important, element in his treatment of the tragic character is more easily discernible. The issue is not psychological but moral. Brutus is honest, intellectually and all-otherwise. So far as conduct in this life can be guided by principles, his is so guided. And yet it must certainly be thought that the decision on the ground of these principles to kill Caesar was not easily or speedily arrived at, and there is no reason to suppose (and no evidence) that a certain "fumbling" in the decisive soliloquy in any way implies a specific impurity of motive. A man may be sure of his principles and doubtful of their exercise. This "fumbling," this uncertainty, is premonitory evidence of the moral issue of the play, so far as Brutus is concerned in it; that the moral decision must be made, but that even in the making of it and whatever the decision may be, Brutus will be involved in moral error. This error is no specific impurity, such as unlawful or even unconscious ambition; it is an error inherent in the decision itself, in all decisions, even in their "honesty." There could perhaps be no more significant comment on the relation between the private moral judgement and the apprehension of all political order whatsoever. It is a terrible thought but a true one: the statesman is never right, but to choose the right he must continually endeavour. And this is true of every man, in all moral activity.

It must not be thought, however, that succeeding external events only prove him wrong—the fickleness of the Roman mob, the extortion of money by Cassius, imminent defeat—they merely suggest the bewildering truth, but it is a truth not dependent on temporal occasions. External events cast an ironical shadow over the honesty of Brutus, and we marvel that in such good could be mixed such evil. As Brutus's fortunes decline our moral vision grows more widely comprehending, but it is no argument from failure that makes us question the earlier decision. It is not merely failure that deepens that vision with the recognition that attachment to honesty may be attachment to my honesty, and that it is not only Brutus's honesty that is impugned but all mortal honesty whatsoever. To find the flaw in this honesty in something particular to the act, making it dishonest, is to destroy the meaning of the play. For the study of Brutus is a study in that evil original in our flesh which brings in a little corruption—and often more than a little—whenever man, in decision and action, addresses himself, as he must, to his world.

"Or Else Were This a Savage Spectacle"

by Brents Stirling

Modern readers are prone to find the tragedy of Brutus in his rigid devotion to justice and fair play. Many members of the Globe audience, however, believed that his virtues were complicated by self-deception and doubtful principle. In sixteenth-century views of history the conspiracy against Caesar often represented a flouting of unitary sovereignty, that prime point of Tudor policy, and exemplified the anarchy thought to accompany "democratic" or constitutional checks upon authority. Certain judgments of Elizabethan political writers who refer to Brutus are quite clear upon this point.[1] Although naturally aware of his disinterested honor and liberality, contemporary audiences could thus perceive in him a conflict between questionable goals and honorable action, a contradiction lying in his attempt to redeem morally confused ends by morally clarified means. The Elizabethan tragedy of Brutus, like that of Othello, is marked by an integrity of conduct which leads the protagonist into evil and measures him in his error.

The distinction between modern and Elizabethan views of *Julius Caesar* is not the point of our inquiry, but it is a necessary beginning, for the older view of Brutus determines both the symbolic quality and the structure of the play. I hope to show that a sixteenth-century idea

---

[1] See the discussion in J. E. Phillips's *The State in Shakespeare's Greek and Roman Plays* (New York, 1940), pp. 172ff. Mr. Phillips quotes at length from such typical spokesmen as Sir Thomas Elyot and Thomas Craig. His analysis of *Julius Caesar* on this basis is also illuminating. See also the present author's *The Populace in Shakespeare* (New York, 1949), p. 147, for a condemnation by William Covell of Romans who aroused civil dissension by covering their purposes "with the fine terms of a common good, of the freedom of the people, of justice. . . ." The parallel with Brutus is a very close one, and Covell, moreover, explicitly avows a topical relation of such Roman history to the civil tensions of Elizabethan England.

of Brutus is as thoroughly related to Shakespeare's art as it is to his meaning.

When a dramatist wishes to present an idea, his traditional method, of course, is to settle upon an episode in which the idea arises naturally but vividly from action and situation. Such an episode in *Julius Caesar* is the one in which Brutus resolves to exalt not only the mission but the tactics of conspiracy: having accepted republicanism as an honorable end, he sets out to dignify assassination, the means, by lifting it to a level of rite and ceremony.[2] In II. i, as Cassius urges the killing of Antony as a necessary accompaniment to the death of Caesar, Brutus declares that "such a course will seem too bloody . . . ,/ To cut the head off and then hack the limbs." With this thought a sense of purpose comes over him: "Let's be sacrificers, but not butchers, Caius." Here his conflict seems to be resolved, and for the first time he is more than a reluctant presence among the conspirators as he expands the theme which ends his hesitation and frees his moral imagination:

> We all stand up against the spirit of Caesar,
> And in the spirit of men there is no blood;
> Oh, that we then could come by Caesar's spirit,
> And not dismember Caesar! But, alas,
> Caesar must bleed for it! And, gentle friends,
> Let's kill him boldly, but not wrathfully;
> Let's carve him as a dish fit for the gods,
> Not hew him as a carcass fit for hounds.

This proposed conversion of bloodshed to ritual is the manner in which an abstract Brutus will be presented in terms of concrete art. From the suggestion of Plutarch that Brutus' first error lay in sparing Antony, Shakespeare moves to the image of Antony as a limb of Caesar, a limb not to be hacked because hacking is no part of ceremonial sacrifice. From Plutarch's description of Brutus as high-minded, gentle and disinterested, Shakespeare proceeds to the Brutus of symbolic action. Gentleness and disinterestedness become embodied in the act of "unwrathful" blood sacrifice. High-mindedness becomes objectified in ceremonial observance.

A skeptical reader may ask why the episode just described is any

[2] My article on the ritual theme in *Julius Caesar* (*PMLA*, LXVI, pp. 765ff.) appeared in 1951 as an early draft of this chapter. Some of my principal observations have been repeated by Ernest Schanzer in a recent essay ("The Tragedy of Shakespeare's Brutus," *ELH* (March, 1955), pp. 1ff.; see pp. 6–8).

more significant than a number of others such as Brutus' scene with Portia or his quarrel with Cassius. If more significant, it is so only because of its relation to a thematic design. I agree, moreover, that Shakespeare gains his effects by variety; as a recognition, in fact, of his complexity I hope to show that the structure of *Julius Caesar* is marked by reference both varied and apt to Brutus' sacrificial rite, and that this process includes expository preparation in earlier scenes, emphasis upon "mock-ceremony" in both earlier and later scenes, and repeated comment by Antony upon butchery under the guise of sacrifice—ironical comment which takes final form in the parley before Philippi.

Derived in large measure from Plutarch, but never mechanically or unselectively, the theme of incantation and ritual is thus prominent throughout *Julius Caesar,* and this is no less true at the beginning than during the crucial episodes of Acts II and III. In the opening scene of the play we are confronted with a Roman populace rebuked by Marullus for ceremonial idolatry of Caesar:

> And do you now put on your best attire?
> And do you now cull out a holiday?
> And do you now strew flowers in his way
> That comes in triumph over Pompey's blood?

For this transgression Marullus prescribes a counter-observance by the citizens in immediate expiation of their folly:

> Run to your houses, fall upon your knees,
> Pray to the gods to intermit this plague
> That needs must light on this ingratitude.

To which Flavius adds:

> Go, go, good countrymen, and for this fault,
> Assemble all the poor men of your sort;
> Draw them to Tiber banks, and weep your tears
> Into the channel, till the lowest stream
> Do kiss the most exalted shores of all.

And after committing the populace to these rites of atonement for their festal celebration of Caesar, the two tribunes themselves leave to remove the devotional symbols set up for his welcoming. "Go you . . . towards the Capitol;/ This way will I. Disrobe the images/ If you do find them decked with ceremonies./ . . . let no images/ Be hung with Caesar's trophies." It is the hope of Flavius that these disenchantments will make Caesar "fly an ordinary pitch,/ Who else would soar above the view of men."

Act I, scene ii is equally unusual in carrying the theme of ritual. It is apparent that Shakespeare had a wide choice of means for staging the entry of Caesar and his retinue; yet he selects an entry based upon Plutarch's description of the "feast Lupercalia" in which the rite of touching or striking barren women by runners of the course is made prominent. Caesar, moreover, after ordering Calpurnia to be so touched by Antony, commands: "Set on; and leave no ceremony out." It can be said, in fact, that the whole of this scene is written with ceremonial observance as a background. Its beginning, already described, is followed by a touch of solemnity in the soothsayer's words; next comes its main expository function, the sounding of Brutus by Cassius, and throughout this interchange come at intervals the shouts and flourishes of a symbolic spectacle. When the scene is again varied by a formal reentry and exit of Caesar's train, Casca remains behind to make a mockery of the rite which has loomed so large from off-stage. Significantly, in Casca's travesty of the ceremonial crown-offering and of the token offering by Caesar of his throat for cutting, Shakespeare has added a satirical note which does not appear in Plutarch.

The process, then, in each of the two opening episodes has been the bringing of serious ritual into great prominence, and of subjecting it to satirical treatment. In the first scene the tribunes denounce the punctilio planned for Caesar's entry, send the idolatrous crowd to rites of purification, and set off themselves to desecrate the devotional images. In the second scene a multiple emphasis of ceremony is capped by Casca's satire which twists the crown ritual into imbecile mummery. At this point, and in conformity with the mood set by Casca, occurs Cassius' mockery in soliloquy of Brutus:

> Well, Brutus, thou art noble; yet I see
> Thy honorable mettle may be wrought
> From that it is dispos'd; therefore it is meet
> That noble minds keep ever with their likes;
> For who is so firm that cannot be seduc'd?

The next scene (I. iii) is packed with omens and supernatural portents, a note which is carried directly into II. i where Brutus, on receiving the mysterious papers which have been left to prompt his action, remarks,

> The exhalations whizzing in the air
> Give so much light that I may read by them.

Appropriately, the letters read under this weird glow evoke his first real commitment to the "cause":

> O Rome, I make thee promise
> If the redress will follow, thou receivest
> Thy full petition at the hand of Brutus!

Now appear his lines on the interim "between the acting of a dreadful thing/ And the first motion" in which "the state of man/ Like to a little kingdom, suffers then/ The nature of a insurrection." This conventional symbolizing of political convulsion by inward insurrection is followed by the soliloquy on conspiracy:

> O, then by day
> Where wilt thou find a cavern dark enough
> To mask thy monstrous visage? Seek none, Conspiracy!
> Hide it in smiles and affability.

The conflict within Brutus thus becomes clear in this scene. First, the participant in revolution suffers revolution within himself; then the hater of conspiracy and lover of plain dealing must call upon Conspiracy to hide in smiling courtesy.

We have now reached the critical point (II. i. 154ff.) to which attention was first called, an outward presentation of Brutus' crisis through his acceptance of an assassin's role upon condition that the assassins become sacrificers. Already a theme well established in preceding scenes, the idea of ritual is again made prominent. As the soliloquy on conspiracy closes, the plotters gather, and the issue becomes the taking of an oath. Brutus rejects this as an idle ceremony unsuited to men joined in the honesty of a cause and turns now to the prospect of Caesar's death. This time, however, honorable men do need ceremony, ceremony which will purify the violent act of all taint of butchery and raise it to the level of sacrifice. But although Brutus has steadied himself with a formula his conflict is still unresolved, for as he sets his course he "unconsciously" reveals the evasion which Antony later will amplify: to transmute political killing into ritual is to cloak it with appearances. We began with Brutus' passage on carving Caesar as a dish for the gods; these are the lines which complete it:

> And let our hearts, as subtle masters do,
> Stir up their servants to an act of rage,
> And after seem to chide 'em. This shall make
> Our purpose necessary and not envious;

Which so appearing to the common eyes,
We shall be called purgers, not murderers.

The contradiction is interesting. In an anticlimax, Brutus has ended his great invocation to ritual with a note on practical politics: our hearts shall stir us and afterward seem to chide us; we shall thus "appear" to the citizenry as purgers, not murderers.

Shakespeare never presents Brutus as a demagogue, but there are ironical traces of the politician in him which suggest Covell's adverse picture of Roman liberators.[3] It is curious, in fact, that although Brutus is commonly thought to be unconcerned over public favor, he expresses clear concern for it in the passage just quoted and in III. i. 244–51, where he sanctions Antony's funeral speech only if Antony agrees to tell the crowd that he speaks by generous permission, and only if he agrees to utter no evil of the conspiracy. Nor is Brutus' speech in the Forum wholly the nonpolitical performance it is supposed to be; certainly Shakespeare's Roman citizens are the best judges of it, and they react tempestuously. Although compressed, it scarcely discloses aloofness or an avoidance of popular emotive themes.

Act II, scene ii now shifts to the house of Caesar, but the emphasis on ritual continues as before. With dramatic irony, in view of Brutus' recent lines on sacrificial murder, Caesar commands, "Go bid the priests do present sacrifice." Calpurnia who has "never stood on ceremonies" (omens) is now terrified by them. News comes that the augurers, plucking the entrails of an offering, have failed to find a heart. Calpurnia has dreamed that smiling Romans have laved their hands in blood running from Caesar's statue, and Decius Brutus gives this its favorable interpretation which sends Caesar to his death.

The vivid assassination scene carries out Brutus' ritual prescription in dramatic detail, for the killing is staged with a formalized approach, ending in kneeling, by one conspirator after another until the victim is surrounded. This is met by a series of retorts from Caesar ending in "Hence! Wilt thou lift up Olympus," and the "sacrifice" is climaxed with his "Et tu Brute!" The conspirators ceremonially bathe their hands in Caesar's blood, and Brutus pronounces upon "this our lofty scene" with the prophecy that it "shall be acted over/ In states unborn and accents yet unknown!"

The mockery in counterritual now begins as a servant of Antony enters (III. i. 121) and confronts Brutus:

[3] See the reference and quotation in note 1.

Thus, Brutus, did my master bid me kneel,
Thus did Mark Antony bid me fall down;
And being prostrate, thus he bade me say:
Brutus is noble, wise, valiant, and honest.

Here a threefold repetition, "kneel," "fall down," and "being prostrate," brings the ceremonial irony close to satire. Following this worship of the new idol by his messenger, Antony appears in person and with dramatic timing offers himself as a victim. In one speech he evokes both the holy scene which the conspirators so desired and the savagery which underlay it:

Now, whilst your purpled hands do reek and smoke,
Fulfill your pleasure. Live a thousand years,
I shall not find myself so apt to die;
No place will please me so, no mean of death,
As here by Caesar, and by you cut off.

The murder scene is thus hallowed by Antony in a manner which quite reverses its sanctification by the conspirators. Brutus, forbearing, attempts to mollify Antony with his cherished theme of purgation:

Our hearts you see not. They are pitiful,
And pity to the general wrong of Rome—
As fire drives out fire, so pity pity—
Hath done this deed on Caesar.

Antony's response is again one of counterceremony, the shaking of hands in formal sequence which serves to make each conspirator stand alone and unprotected by the rite of blood which had united him with the others. The assassins had agreed as a token of solidarity that each of them should stab Caesar. Antony seems to allude to this:

Let each man render me his bloody hand.
First, Marcus Brutus, will I shake with you;
Now, Caius Cassius, do I take your hand;
Now, Decius Brutus, yours; now yours, Mettellus;
Yours, Cinna; and, my valiant Casca, yours;
Though last, not least in love yours, good Trebonius.
Gentlemen all—alas what shall I say?

It is then that Antony, addressing the body of Caesar, suddenly delivers his first profanation of the ritual sacrifice:

Here wast thou bay'd brave hart;
Here didst thou fall; and here thy hunters stand,
Sign'd in thy spoil, and crimson'd in thy lethe.

And lest the allusion escape, Shakespeare continues Antony's inversion of Brutus' ceremonial formula: the dish carved for the gods is doubly transformed into the carcass hewn for hounds with further hunting metaphors of Caesar as a hart in the forest and as "a deer strucken by many princes." Brutus agrees to give reasons why Caesar was dangerous, "or else were this a savage spectacle," and the stage is set for what may be called the play's chief counterritual. Only Brutus, who planned the rite of sacrifice, could with such apt irony arrange the "true rites" and "ceremonies" which are to doom the conspiracy.

> I will myself into the pulpit first
> And show the reason of our Caesar's death.
> What Antony shall speak, I will protest
> He speaks by leave and by permission,
> And that we are contented Caesar shall
> Have all true rites and lawful ceremonies.

But exactly after the manner of his speech announcing the ritual sacrifice (II. i) Brutus concludes again on a note of policy: "It shall advantage more than do us wrong."

Next follows Antony *solus* rendering his prophecy of "domestic fury and fierce civil strife" symbolized in Caesar's ghost which will

> Cry "Havoc," and let slip the dogs of war,
> That this foul deed shall smell above the earth.

The passage is similar in utterance, function, and dramatic placement to Carlisle's prophecy on the deposition of Richard II, and for that reason it is to be taken seriously as a choric interpretation of Caesar's death. Significantly, the beginning lines again deride Brutus' erstwhile phrase, "sacrificers but not butchers":

> O, pardon me, thou bleeding piece of earth,
> That I am meek and gentle with these butchers!

It is unnecessary to elaborate upon the Forum scene; Antony's oration follows the speech of Brutus with consequences familiar to all readers. But there is an element in Antony's turning of the tables which is just as remarkable as the well-known irony of his references to "honorable men." If we remember that Shakespeare has emphasized ritual at various planes of seriousness and of derision, the conclusion of Antony's speech to the populace will link itself with the previous theme. For here Antony reenacts the death of Caesar in a ritual of his own, one intended to show that the original "lofty scene" presented a base carnage. Holding Caesar's bloody mantle as a talisman, he reproduces *seriatim* the sacrificial strokes, but he does so in terms of the "rent" Casca made and the "cursed steel" that Brutus plucked away with the blood of Caesar following it. Again, each conspirator had struck individually at Caesar and had symbolically involved himself with the others; for the second time Antony reminds us of this ritual bond by recounting each stroke, and his recreation of the rite becomes a mockery of it. Brutus' transformation of blood into the heady wine of sacrifice is reversed both in substance and in ceremony.

For the "realists" among the conspirators what has occurred can be summed up in the bare action of the play: the killing of Caesar has been accomplished, but the fruits of it have been spoiled by Brutus' insistence that Antony live and that he speak at Caesar's funeral. "The which," as North's Plutarch has it, "marred all." With reference to Brutus, however, something much more significant has been enacted; the "insurrection," the contradiction, within him has taken outward form in his attempt to purify assassination through ceremony. This act, not to be found in Plutarch,[4] symbolizes the "Elizabethan" Brutus compelled by honor to join with conspirators but required by conscience to reject Conspiracy.

[4] A reference at this point to Plutarch will serve both to clarify my meaning and to allay some natural doubts concerning the dramatist's intention. While it is true that the ritual murder of Caesar is Shakespeare's own contribution, the expository preparation for it in Act I comes from an episode in Plutarch in which Antony concludes the Lupercalian rites by offering a laurel crown twice to Caesar, and in which the tribunes are described as desecrating ritual offerings (*Shakespeare's Plutarch,* I, 92–3; see also II, 19–20). Hence we have basic ritual materials for Shakespeare's first two scenes present in one convenient block of his source which also offered a convenient beginning for the play. Does this prevent us from attaching significance to the unusual presence of ritual elements in the exposition scenes? I believe it does not, for two reasons. First, the choice of source material by a dramatist is itself significant; Shakespeare could have started the play with other episodes in Plutarch or with scenes of his own invention. Secondly, it is immaterial whether he began *Julius Caesar* with this episode in his source and, because of its wealth of ritual detail, was led to the theme of ritualized assassination, or whether he began with the theme and chose source materials for exposition which agreed with it. In either case the same remarkable unity between earlier and later parts of the play would have been achieved, and it is this unity which is important. Guesses about its origin in the playwright's composition are profitless. We do know that Shakespeare's Brutus plans the killing of Caesar as ritual, while Plutarch presents it as the very opposite of this. Plutarch's description of the assassination emphasizes, in fact, resemblance to the hunting down of an animal, the very effect Brutus seeks explicitly to avoid in the "carcass-hounds" figure, and the one which Antony magnifies in his counteremphasis of imagery drawn from hunting. North notes it thus:

We have followed the ritual theme in *Julius Caesar* from early scenes to the point of Antony's oration, at which it is completely defined. There remains, however, a terminal appearance of the theme in the first scene of Act V. The ultimate clash between the idealism of Brutus and Antony's contempt for it comes during the parley on the eve of Philippi, at which Antony again drives home the old issue of ceremonial imposture. Brutus has observed that his enemy wisely threats before he stings; the reply is Antony's last disposition of the sacrificial rite:

> Villains, you did not so when your vile daggers
> Hack'd one another in the sides of Caesar,
> You show'd your teeth like apes, and fawn'd like hounds,
> And bow'd like bondmen, kissing Caesar's feet;
> Whilst damned Casca, like a cur, behind
> Struck Caesar on the neck.

Antony invokes the "hacking" which Brutus earlier foreswore, and he again inverts the cherished formula of sacrifice: once more the dish carved for gods becomes the carcass hewn for hounds. Over the body of Caesar he had previously employed the hunting-hound figure ("Here wast thou bay'd, brave hart."); the apes, the hounds, and the cur of these lines complete his vengeful irony of metaphor.

What, finally, is to be inferred from Antony's concluding passage on "the noblest Roman of them all"? Commonly found there is a broad vindication of Brutus which would deny an ironical interpretation. When Antony's elegiac speech is read plainly, however, its meaning is quite limited: it declares simply that Brutus was the only conspirator untouched by envy, and that, in intention, he acted "in a general honest thought/ And common good to all." The Elizabethan view of Brutus as tragically misguided is thus consistent with Anthony's pronouncement that he was the only disinterested member of the conspiracy. But Brutus is not to be summed up in an epitaph; as the impersonal member of a conspiracy motivated largely by personal ends, he sought in a complex way to resolve his contradiction by depersonalizing, ritualizing, the means.

Shakespeare's achievement, however, is not confined to the characterization of a major figure, for we have seen that the ceremonial

---

"Caesar turned him nowhere but he was stricken at by some . . . and was hacked and mangled among them, as a wild beast taken of hunters." (*Shakespeare's Plutarch*, I, 101–2.)

motive extends beyond the personality of Brutus into the structure of the play. Exposition stressing the idea of ritual observance leads to the episode in which Brutus formulates the "sacrifice," and clear resolution of the idea follows in event and commentary. Structural craftsmanship thus supplements characterization and the two combine, as in *Richard II,* to state the political philosophy implicit in the play.

Shakespeare and Political Wisdom: A Note on the Personalism of *Julius Caesar*

by L. C. Knights

The land is mark'd for desolation & unless we plant
The seeds of Cities & of Villages in the Human bosom
Albion must be a rock of blood.

Blake, *Jerusalem*: IV

It is no use pretending that poets can give direct answers to political problems ("We have no gift to set a statesman right," said Yeats, truly). Nor is a knowledge of literature, however extensive, a substitute for a knowledge of the complex circumstances that make up a particular political problem. Yet if we believe that great literature has something to say about the human situation, that it is great precisely because of its grasp of what man is or may be, then we are surely committed to believing that our knowledge of literature, what we know *from* literature, has some bearing, however indirect, on our thinking about politics. In this essay I shall try to show how Shakespeare, without solving any "problems" for us, can nourish our thinking about the perennial issues of politics. The plays I want to look at, *Julius Caesar* and *Coriolanus*, have, it is true, an overt political content, but in the manner of their working they are, I think, representative of a wide range of literature.

An important part of the imaginative impact of *Julius Caesar* lies in our awareness of a contrast between public life and private. This has been variously noted. Commentators point to the ironic contrast be-

---

"Shakespeare and Political Wisdom: A Note on the Personalism of Julius Caesar*" by L. C. Knights. From* Sewanee Review, *LXI (1953), 43–48, 53–55. Copyrighted by The University of the South. Reprinted by permission of the author and publisher.*

tween Caesar the public figure and Caesar the man ("Come on my right hand, for this ear is deaf"). When Brutus, in his "gown"—the symbol of domestic privacy[1]—speaks gently to his boy, we are told that this "relieves the strain" of the tragic action. And every account of the characters includes some reference to those aspects of Caesar, Brutus and Cassius that are revealed in their more intimate moments and hidden or disguised in public. What seems not to be recognized is the cumulative effect of these and many other reminders of a more personal life—the important part this pervasive but unobtrusive personalism plays, or should play, in our evaluation of the public action.

That we are intended to be aware of the characters as men, of the faces behind the masks, is clear enough. Not only are all the main figures at some time divested of their robes—those "robes and furr'd gowns" that, according to King Lear, "hide all"—and allowed to appear as husbands, masters of households, and friends, but they all in turn emphasize each other's personal characteristics. A principal reason why Cassius thinks that Caesar isn't fit for his exalted position is that he, Cassius, is the stronger swimmer, and that Caesar, like the rest of us, was hot and cold and thirsty when he had a fever. And although Antony deliberately makes emotional capital out of Caesar's mantle,

> I remember
> The first time Caesar ever put it on;
> 'Twas on a summer's evening, in his tent. . . .

the touch of particularity, of revealed privacy, is intended for us, the audience, as well as for the Roman crowd. We notice too how often the verb "love" appears in this play, how often different characters speak of their love—their "dear love" or "their kind love"—for each other, how often they seem to find a special satisfaction in referring to themselves as "brothers." Now the effect of all this is not only one of pathos or simple irony. The focus of our attention is the public world: from the arena of that world, personal life—where truth between man and man resides—is glimpsed as across a gulf. The distance between these two worlds is the measure of the distortion and falsity that takes place in the attempt to make "politics" self-enclosed.

The attempt is common to both sides. Caesar constantly assumes the public mask:

[1] In II, ii the contrast is emphasized in visual terms. "Enter Caesar in his night-gown" (a dressing-gown or house-coat). Then, as the conspirators prevail over his wife's entreaties (l.107), "Give me my robe, for I will go."

So in the world; 'tis furnish'd well with men,
And men are flesh and blood, and apprehensive;
Yet in the number I do know but one
That unassailable holds on his rank,
Unshak'd of motion: and that I am he,

Brutus, who loved Caesar, wrenches his mind to divorce policy from friendship.

It must be by his death: and for my part,
I know no personal cause to spurn at him,
But for the general. . . .

In the soliloquy from which this comes (II, i) qualities known in direct contact between persons are dismissed as irrelevant to public considerations, and it is precisely this that gives the air of tortuous unreality to Brutus's self-persuadings.

The abuse of greatness is when it disjoins
Remorse from power; and, to speak truth of Caesar,
I have not known when his affections sway'd
More than his reason. . . .
[But] since the quarrel
Will bear no colour for the thing he is,
Fashion it thus. . . .

It is by such sophistries[2] that Brutus launches himself on what Clarendon was to call "that fathomless abyss of Reason of State."

What the play also makes manifest, however, is that personal feelings, which Brutus tries to exclude from his deliberations on "the general good," are in fact active in public life. But they are active in the wrong way. Unacknowledged, they influence simply by distorting. We need not make much of the slanging-match between the generals before Philippi; but the famous quarrel-scene between Brutus and Cassius certainly has this ironic significance. It is of course Cassius, in whom the "taboo on tenderness" [3] is strongest—who is scornful of "our mothers' spirits" (I, iii, 83) and despises Caesar for behaving "as a sick girl" (I, ii, 127)—who here displays the most pronounced "feminine"

[2] On which Coleridge shrewdly comments, "he would have no objection to a king, or to Caesar, a monarch in Rome, would Caesar but be as good a monarch as he now seems disposed to be!" But Coleridge found this defective reasoning perplexing, as being "discordant with our historical preconceptions of Brutus." *Lectures on Shakespeare* (Bohn's Popular Library), p. 313.

[3] The phrase is Ian Suttie's. See *The Origins of Love and Hate.*

traits, "that rash humour which my mother gave me" (IV, iii, 119). That the whole thing contrives to be touching should not obscure the fact that the questions at issue did demand a more impersonal consideration. And it is above all in Cassius that the springs of political action are revealed as only too personal. What nags at him is simply envy of Caesar,

> A man no mightier than thyself or me
> In personal action, yet prodigious grown.

We get the impression that his appeals to Roman "honour," to the "nobility" of his associates, are not simply laid on for the benefit of Brutus, but are part of his own self-deception. The banished feelings have simply come in by the back door, thinly disguised.

> Tempting region that
> For Zeal to enter and refresh herself
> Where passions had the privilege to work
> And never hear the sound of their own names.[4]

The moral *dérèglement,* the confusion of values and priorities, issues in a kind of masquerade, as when the forms of friendship are exploited for political ends.[5] It is this that explains our sense of something monstrous in the action, imperfectly symbolized by the storm and prodigies, and made explicit by Brutus in soliloquy when, deserting the actual, he has given himself to a phantasmagoria of abstractions.

> Between the acting of a dreadful thing
> And the first motion, all the interim is
> Like a phantasma or a hideous dream. . . .
> O conspiracy!
> Sham'st thou to show thy dangerous brow by night,
> When evils are most free? O! then by day
> Where wilt thou find a cavern dark enough
> To mask thy monstrous visage? Seek none, conspiracy;
> Hide it in smiles and affability:
> For if thou path, thy native semblance on,
> Not Erebus itself were dim enough
> To hide thee from prevention.

[4] Wordsworth, *The Prelude,* XI, 228–231.

[5] Decius enveigles Caesar with protestations of "dear dear love," and the conspirators drink wine with their victim before leading him to the Capitol; Brutus kisses Caesar immediately before the killing; Antony talks much of love and shakes hands all round as a way of deceiving the conspirators.

But the "phantasma," far from ending with the death of Caesar, extends beyond it. We are made aware not only of a complete lack of correspondence between the professed intentions of the conspirators and the result of their act, but of the *unreality* of the world which they inhabit. The incongruity between intention and effect is ironically underlined in the excited proclamations after the murder,

> And, waving our red weapons o'er our heads,
> Let's all cry "Peace, freedom, and liberty,"

for the upshot of course is neither peace nor republican liberty. The slackened grasp on reality is emphasized by the sombre comedy of Brutus's oration: so far as addressing real people is concerned he might as well have kept quiet ("Let him be Caesar"). In the last act the conspirators appear almost as automata. (If it is "stoicism" that prevents Brutus from mourning his wife, then stoicism is a very dubious attitude.) Committed to the public world, the public world has failed them, and nothing is left but some nostalgic memories and a desire for death. It is the touching incongruity of the memories—"This is my birth-day," "Thou know'st that we two went to school together"—the moving expression, so many times repeated, of the need for friendship that, by emphasizing the reality of personal life and at the same time removing it to a great distance, completes the pattern of the play. For it is the intolerable divorce between public life and the trust, loyalty and affection that men look for in personal living that explains the barrenness of action that is purely public and political, just as it is the major reason why, in this play, men

> construe things after their fashion,
> Clean from the purpose of the things themselves. . . .

The simple conclusions that I wish to draw are probably by now sufficiently obvious, but when one is in earnest one may as well be explicit. Neither *Julius Caesar* nor *Coriolanus* can be summed up in a moral formula. But, taken together, they point to two related truths of the greatest importance. The first is that human actuality is more important than *any* political abstraction, though more difficult to bear. The second is that politics is vitiated and corrupted to the extent to which, as politicians, we lose our sense of the *person* on the other side of the dividing line of class or party or nation. Both plays—and especially *Coriolanus*—refresh our sense of the actual where today it is most urgently needed.

The point is worth insisting on. There has probably never been a time when social and political thinking has moved so glibly, with so little check, in the realm of the abstract. In England we think in terms of productivity curves, of "targets" achieved or missed, of the rationalization of industry, of the educational ladder, and so on. Such abstractions are necessary in certain contexts and for certain purposes. The trouble arises when, by constant bandying about, they simply stand opaquely between us and the specific human content, the kind and quality of individual lives, that they are intended to cover. When the cliché phrases become invested with emotion and we cling to them as banners (or savage them as red rags), then whatever we may be doing when we air our views we are certainly not contributing to the health of the state. ("General good," said Blake with some exaggeration, "is the cry of the hypocrite and the scoundrel"; adding, with no exaggeration at all, "he who would do good to another must do it in minute particulars.")

In party and international politics the dangers of abstraction, or—to speak more correctly—of impure quasi-abstraction, are even more plain to see, since it is here that passions from unacknowledged sources are most readily enlisted. "This was the time," says Wordsworth, speaking of his period of Godwinian speculation, in the passage of *The Prelude* to which I have already referred,

> This was the time, when, all things tending fast
> To depravation, speculative schemes—
> That promised to abstract the hopes of Man
> Out of his feelings, to be fixed thenceforth
> For ever in a purer element—
> Found ready welcome. Tempting region *that*
> For Zeal to enter and refresh herself,
> Where passions had the privilege to work,
> And never hear the sound of their own names.

And of course there are grosser forms than Godwinian enthusiasms and revolutionary ardors. There is no need, however, to instance the simpler forms of psychological "projection" which explain so much in the daily press (the ogres always the same, and always in the same stock attitudes). The point is that whenever thought moves in terms of the massive abstractions of "progressive parties," of "anti-Fascism," of "the American way of life," of "people's democracies," of Socialist virtue and Tory viciousness (or vice versa), it needs to be brought back to the discipline of the actual. It is not our political shibboleths but the decency and integrity of our human responsiveness that in the not so long run decides the fate of nations.

These of course are commonplaces, but they belong to the class of commonplaces that Coleridge described—"Truths, of all others the most awful and interesting . . . too often considered as *so* true, that they lose all the power of truth, and lie bed-ridden in the dormitory of the soul, side by side with the most despised and exploded errors." [6] Literature can help experience to re-vivify them.

[6] *The Friend,* Essay XV, *Aids to Reflection,* p. 1.

Language and Action in *Julius Caesar*

by R. A. Foakes

These various themes in language and action all suggest a full circle of events in the play, civil war leading to civil war, blood to blood, imaged in the beginning and close of a day. They form a large part of the play's imaginative framework, and perhaps indicate that the structural unity of *Julius Caesar* lies in the birth and completion of the rebellion. If this view is taken, there is no need to go beyond the play into *Antony and Cleopatra* in order to explain it, to see the spirit of Caesar as a fate against which Brutus strives in vain, or to see the play as a kind of revenge tragedy.[1]

At the same time this view of the play as being about faction, and the waste and destruction that attends it, calls for a reassessment of the main characters. For Caesar, Brutus and Cassius, in spite of their different natures and functions, are equal participants. The conspirators stand up against the spirit of Caesar, which only finds rest in their deaths, so that in a sense the death of Brutus and Cassius is the death of Caesar also. These three figures share the main action of the play, which culminates in their destruction; Antony and Octavius are left to provide continuity, to suggest the life that carries on. In this main action, the rebellion, Brutus does not appear a tragic hero, as he is so often made out to be, nor does Caesar appear a villain, a tyrant-dictator.[2] Brutus believes in an ideal, honor, but confuses it with treachery; Caesar maintains an ideal vision of himself as necessary to his position;

"Language and Action in Julius Caesar." *From "An Approach to* Julius Caesar" *by R. A. Foakes,* Shakespeare Quarterly, *V (1954), 263–70. Reprinted by permission of the author and The Shakespeare Association of America, Inc.*

[1] See J. E. Phillips Jr., *The State in Shakespeare's Greek and Roman Plays* (1940), p. 174; J. Dover Wilson (Editor), *Julius Caesar* (New Cambridge Edition, 1949), p. xxii; J. A. K. Thomson, *Shakespeare and the Classics* (1952), pp. 204–05.

[2] J. Dover Wilson sought to prove that this was the traditional view of Caesar in his New Cambridge edition, but the arguments against have been well put by D. S. Brewer, "'Brutus' Crime': A Footnote to *Julius Caesar*," *R.E.S. New Series,* III (January 1952), 51–54.

Cassius uses the various ideals posited in the play to sway Brutus, to engineer Caesar's murder, and yet himself shares the ideals of liberty and of being a Roman. Brutus and Caesar as men do not measure up to the ideal, and Cassius proves to be nobler than a manipulator, than a mere sketch for Iago.

Once again an examination of the use of language in relation to action amplifies this analysis. The use of rhetoric in the play has often been noticed; repetition, balanced phrasing, formal apostrophes and similes, give a "public" quality to much of the verse, culminating in the orations, which stand out from their context, yet are harmonious with it. By its nature the verse helps to point the contrast between the public figure and the private man. In addition it is hinted that the major characters are acting when in public, notably when Brutus tells the conspirators

> Let not our looks put on our purposes,
> But bear it as our Roman actors do,
> With untired spirits and formal constancy, (II, i, 225–27)

and when, immediately after the murder, Cassius and Brutus in turn speak of the times "this our lofty scene" shall be "acted over" in the future, and Caesar shall "bleed in sport" (III, i, 112ff.).

A more individual rhetorical feature is the device of speaking in the third person, as in Brutus's oration:

> Brutus' love to Caesar was no less than his. If then that friend demand why Brutus rose against Caesar. . . . (III, ii, 20–22)

This device puts a distance between the speaker and what he is saying, makes his words impersonal,[3] and it is a feature of Caesar's speeches that he speaks in this way:

> Speak; Caesar is turn'd to hear. (I, ii, 17)

> Yet Caesar shall go forth; for these predictions
> Are to the world in general as to Caesar. (II, ii, 28–29)

[3] It is notable that Brutus, who maintains his dignity and distance in his oration, uses the device, but Antony, who descends from the pulpit, mingles with the crowd, and pretends to be a "plain, blunt man" in contrast to the "orator" Brutus (III, ii, 221–222), speaks in his own person. Professor Allardyce Nicoll, to whom I am indebted for his advice, points out that this device is used in other plays, as by Othello (III, iii, 357; V, ii, 291) and Hamlet (I, v, 185; V, ii, 244). In these plays it occurs infrequently and for special purposes, but emphasis on the worth of a name is by no means confined to *Julius Caesar*.

> Caesar should be a beast without a heart,
> If he should stay at home to-day for fear.
> No, Caesar shall not: danger knows full well
> That Caesar is more dangerous than he. (II, ii, 42–45)
>
> Shall Caesar send a lie? (II, ii, 65)

Caesar speaks in this way even in conversation with Calphurnia, but the contrast between the public figure, the name, the ideal, "know, Caesar doth not wrong" (III, i, 47), Caesar on whose face "things that threaten'd" dare not look (II, ii. 10), Caesar as "unshaked of motion" (III, i, 70), constant as the northern star (III, i, 60), and the private citizen, Caesar as deaf, subject to the falling-sickness, inclined to be superstitious, continually appears:

> I rather tell thee what is to be fear'd
> Than what I fear; for always I am Caesar. (I, ii, 211–212)

The other important characters, especially Brutus and Cassius speak sometimes in a similar way, as in the following examples:

> Brutus had rather be a villager . . . (I, ii, 172)
>
> You speak to Casca, and to such a man . . . (I, iii, 116)
>
> Cassius from bondage will deliver Cassius (I, iii, 90)
>
> To see thy Antony making his peace . . . (III, i, 197)
>
> Revenge yourselves alone on Cassius,
> For Cassius is aweary of the world (IV, iii, 94–95)
>
> think not, thou noble Roman,
> That ever Brutus will go bound to Rome. (V, i, 111–12)

Names are thus important in themselves, being marks of the lineage and standing of a character, and indicating the qualities and virtues the character ought to have, though not necessarily those he actually possesses. So Caesar does not fear Cassius,

> Yet if my name were liable to fear (I, ii, 199)

he would avoid no man sooner; Caesar may be afraid in himself, but his name, his reputation must be impervious to fear. Cassius incites Brutus by comparing his name with Caesar's,

> Brutus and Caesar: what should be in that Caesar?
> Why should that name be sounded more than yours?

> Write them together, yours is as fair a name;
> Sound them, it doth become the mouth as well;
> Weigh them, it is as heavy; conjure with 'em,
> Brutus will start a spirit as soon as Caesar. (I, ii, 142–47)

and by throwing papers in at his window speaking of the "great opinion That Rome holds of his name" (I, ii, 322ff.). Before the battle Brutus quarrels with Cassius over a question of bribery,

> The name of Cassius honours this corruption. (IV, iii, 15)

The importance of a man's name is shown vividly when the plebeians seize Cinna the poet in spite of his protests,

> *Cinna.* I am not Cinna the conspirator.
> *4th Citizen.* It is no matter, his name's Cinna; pluck but his name out of his heart, and turn him going. (III, iii, 36–39)

So the soldiers who capture Lucillius take the name he gives, Brutus, for the person; the name and the ideal, the reputation and the person, are identified in public, but the differences between them are clear to the audience; Caesar the man is less powerful than his name, and Brutus less honorable than his reputation, or his great ancestry,

> There was a Brutus once that would have brook'd
> The eternal devil to keep his state in Rome (I, ii, 159–60)

> My ancestors did from the streets of Rome
> The Tarquin drive, when he was call'd a king, (II, i, 53–54)

and the crowd's shout "Give him a statue with his ancestors" (III, ii, 54) after Brutus's funeral speech carries irony. The contrast is apparent also in the character of Portia, who proudly calls herself

> A woman well reputed, Cato's daughter, (II, i, 295)

yet has to confess in private that she is after all but a weak woman (II, iv, 39).

The names of Caesar (211 times), Brutus (130 times), and to a much lesser degree Cassius (69 times) and Antony (68 times) echo through the play,[4] and are used frequently where a pronoun would occur in

[4] A comparison with others plays perhaps emphasizes this importance of names; in *Hamlet,* a very much longer play, the hero's name occurs 85 times according to Bartlett's *Concordance,* in *Macbeth* 42 times, *Othello* 34 times, *Coriolanus* 43 times (30 as Coriolanus; 13 as Caius or Caius Marcius). It may be significant also that in *Antony and Cleopatra,* where the spirit of Caesar is again prominent, names are also prominent, the name of Antony occurring in 116 passages, and that of Caesar

the other tragedies. Besides contributing to the formality and dignity of the play, the names of Caesar and Brutus in particular have their own special meanings. The word Caesar had long been in use to signify an all-conquering, absolute monarch,[5] and is used in the play with this implication:

> *3rd Citizen.* Let him be Caesar.
> *4th Citizen.* Caesar's better parts
> Shall be crown'd in Brutus. (III, ii, 55–56)

Caesar is kingly: at the beginning of the play a crown is offered to him three times, and later it is reported

> The senators to-morrow
> Mean to establish Caesar as a king;
> And he shall wear his crown by sea and land. (I, iii, 86–88)

> The Senate have concluded
> To give this day a crown to mighty Caesar. (II, ii, 93–94)

The main motive for Brutus' rebellion is that Caesar "would be crown'd" (II, i, 12ff.); Caesar is like a lion, the king of beasts, among the herd of Romans (I, ii, 106) and more dangerous than danger,[6]

> We are two lions litter'd in one day. (II, ii, 46)

This "royal Caesar" (III, ii, 249), whom Brutus had wished to kill only in spirit, in name

> O that we then could come by Caesar's Spirit,
> And not dismember Caesar! But alas,
> Caesar must bleed for it! (II, i, 169–71)

lives on in spirit after his death, and as Antony forecasts,

(Octavius and Julius) in 152 passages. This again is a much longer play than *Julius Caesar* and the repetition of names here seems to be a special feature.

[5] Especially in the form "kaiser," see *Oxford English Dictionary* "kaiser" b, where uses are recorded from 1225 onwards, especially in the phrase "king or kaiser"; see also *Oxford English Dictionary* "Caesar" 2 and 2b. Shakespeare elsewhere uses "Caesar" in a generic sense, cf. *3 Henry VI,* III, i, 18, "No bending knee will call thee Caesar now," and *Merry Wives,* I, iii, 9.

[6] It is notable that all the references to lions, in relation to Caesar, or as portents, or in imagery occur in the early part of the play, before Caesar's death; see II, ii, 17; I, iii, 75; II, i, 206. Perhaps it is not going too far to associate Caesar with the "lion in the Captol" (I, ii, 75), and with Casca's

> Against the Capitol I met a lion
> Who glared upon me, and went surly by,
> Without annoying me (I, iii, 20–22)

> Caesar's spirit, ranging for revenge,
> With Ate by his side come hot from hell,
> Shall in these confines with a monarch's voice
> Cry "Havoc," and let slip the dogs of war. (III, i, 270–73)

Besides this linkage with royalty,[7] Caesar's name and the presence of his dead body on the stage during much of Act III, suggest the presence of Caesar's spirit, although the character has only about 130 in a play of about 2,500 lines. The conspirators "stand up against the spirit of Caesar" (II, i, 167) in order to kill him, but are vanquished by that spirit, embodied in the ghost that visits Brutus, and represented in the iteration of the name,

> O Julius Caesar, thou art mighty yet!
> Thy spirit walks abroad, and turns our swords
> In our own proper entrails. (V, iii, 94–96)

Only on the death of Brutus may Caesar "now be still" (V. v. 50).

The name of Brutus has connections already noticed with distinguished ancestors, and also, more prominently, with honor. This is particularly noticeable in the famous lines of Antony's funeral oration, the repeated "Brutus is an honourable man" (III. ii. 87), but on his first appearance Brutus says

> Set honour in one eye and death i' the other,
> And I will look on both indifferently,
> For let the gods so speed me as I love
> The name of honour more than I fear death. (I, ii, 86–89)

The "name of honour" is frequently attributed to him, not least by himself, as when he tells his audience in his oration, "Believe me for mine honour, and have respect to mine honour, that you may believe" (III, ii, 14–15), blames Cassius for selling "the mighty space of our large honours" (IV, iii, 26), and proudly tells Octavius that he could not die "more honourable" (V, i, 60) than on the sword of Brutus. The name of Brutus is equated with honor, and it is appropriate and sufficient for Lucillius to say to the enemy

> When you do find him, or alive or dead,
> He will be found like Brutus, like himself. (V, iv, 24–25)

[7] The last ironical echo of crowning and kingliness comes in the final scenes when a victor's wreath is placed upon the head of the dead Cassius

> Look, whether he have not crown'd dead Cassius! (V, iii, 97)

The names of Caesar and Brutus thus have symbolic qualities, and represent a concept as well as an individual character. Two other names which have much importance are that of Rome and Roman (72 times in the play), and the name of liberty. The fact that he is a Roman should in itself indicate certain qualities in a man:

those sparks of life
That should be in a Roman you do want (I, iii, 57–58)

what other bond
Than secret Romans, that have spoke the word,
And will not palter? (II, i, 124–26)

every drop of blood
That every Roman bears, and nobly bears,
Is guilty of a several bastardy,
If he do break the smallest particle
Of any promise . . . (II, i, 136–40)

. . . show yourselves true Romans (II, i, 223)

Who is here so rude that would not be a Roman? (III, ii, 33)

If that thou be'st a Roman, take it forth. (IV, iii, 103)

Brutus. Now, as you are a Roman, tell me true,
Messenger. Then like a Roman bear the truth I tell.
(IV, iii, 187–88)

There is a contrast between the Roman ideal and Romans in action, as is seen in the behaviour of the conspirators and the plebeians, similar to that between the ideal and the living person represented in Caesar and Brutus. However, it is in the Roman tradition ("this is a Roman's part," V, iii, 89) that Brutus and Cassius commit suicide rather than be taken prisoner, and it is significant that after the end of Act III the words "Rome" and "Roman" occur only in the mouths of the rebels until the final tribute of Antony to Brutus

This was the noblest Roman of them all. (V, v, 68)

The conspirators, especially Brutus and Cassius, associate themselves with Rome as the home of truth, honor, liberty, and manliness;[8]

[8] The concept of manliness is enhanced by contrast with women as characters and in imagery. So Calphurnia fears for Caesar, and Portia, in spite of her boast that

it is by suggesting that Romans are slaves that Cassius incites Brutus to rebel (I, ii, 150ff.; I, iii, 103ff.); it is for Rome, "O Rome, I make thee promise" (II, i, 56), that Brutus joins the conspiracy, and he is conscious of the duties of being a Roman,

> I had rather be a dog, and bay the moon,
> Than such a Roman. (IV, iii, 27–28)

Romans are free-men, to whom Pompey and Caesar bring slaves, and whose servants are bond-men,

> What tributaries follow him to Rome
> To grace in captive bonds his chariot-wheels? (I, i, 38–39)
>
> He hath brought many captives home to Rome (III, ii, 93)
>
> Who is here so base that would be a bondman? (III, ii, 31)
>
> Go show your slaves how choleric you are,
> And make your bondmen tremble. (IV, iii, 43–44)

It is in the name of freedom that Brutus is persuaded to join the conspiracy against Caesar; Cassius speaks of "groaning underneath this age's yoke" (I, ii, 61), but he will deliver himself from bondage, even by that last resort, suicide (I, iii, 90–95); the Romans are slaves, and Caesar would be no tyrant, "no lion, were not Romans hinds" (I, iii, 106). So after the murder of Caesar the conspirators proclaim "Liberty, freedom and enfranchisement" (III, i, 78, 81, 110) and in future ages they shall be called "the men that gave our country liberty" (III, i, 118). In his speech from the pulpit Brutus pleads that the death of Caesar has brought liberty,

> Had you rather Caesar were living, and die all slaves, than that Caesar were dead, to live all free men? (III, ii, 24–26)

Yet just before they stab Caesar, the conspirators who so eagerly stand up for freedom fawn up him with "low-crooked court'sies" (III, i, 43), and as Antony later says, "bow'd like bondmen, kissing Caesar's feet" (V, i, 42). Instead of greater liberty, there are proscriptions and "bills

---

she is "Cato's daughter," and stronger than her sex (II, i, 292ff.), has to confess later

> How weak a thing
> The heart of woman is! (II, iv, 39–40)

Among the sights seen on the eve of Caesar's murder are women "transformed with their fear" (I, iii, 22–24); for other references to the weakness, rashness or "melting spirits" of women, cf. I, iii, 83–84; II, i, 120–22; IV, iii, 120–21.

of outlawry" (IV, i; IV, iii, 173ff.) in Rome, and Brutus and his friends are forced to chance "upon one battle all our liberties" (V, i, 76). Finally Cassius is driven to seek freedom in suicide; Brutus too, who had said he would never "go bound to Rome" (V, i, 112), kills himself, and Strato can reply to Messala's question "Where is thy master?"

> Free from the bondage you are in, Messala. (V, v, 54)

Through this emphasis on names and ideals a continual contrast is drawn between belief and action. Caesar feels he must act in accordance with his name, his royalty, the public ideal, and goes to his death. Brutus believes it is in accordance with his name of honor, and the reputation of his great ancestor who drove Tarquin from Rome (II, i, 51ff.) that he should try to kill the name of Caesar, Caesar's royalty, although he knows that

> the quarrel
> Will bear no colour for the thing he is. (II, i, 28–29)

He acts in the name of one ideal to destroy another, but the action is dishonorable, and the ideal of liberty, an illusion. Cassius too acts and incites Brutus in the name of liberty, but in destroying Caesar the conspirators are not destroying tyranny, for Caesar is no tyrant, but rather the force of order in Rome. The murder is preceded by bodings of disorder in the portents, and followed by still greater disorder, embodied dramatically in the mob that shouts and clamors equally for Pompey, Caesar, Brutus, and Antony, and tears Cinna to pieces simply because of his name; his death is the first of many,

> These many, then, shall die; their names are prick'd. (IV, i, 1)

The conspirators also believe in the name of Rome and Roman as indicating qualities of manliness, and the ability to control passion; and again, though they act in the name of Rome, action and ideal fail to correspond, as we see in the bickering of the quarrel scene, and as the behaviour of the mob continually shows.

This study of the dramatic purposes for which language and imagery are used in *Julius Caesar* suggests solutions for the problems both of style and diction and of the nature and unity of the play. The imagery of words and action points to the imaginative and dramatic unity of the play as consisting in the completion of the circle of events beginning and ending the rebellion. The action of the play turns on the distance between the ideals and public symbols for which the names of Caesar, Brutus, and Cassius, stand, and their true nature and actions. The three main figures are all noble and yet weak; none has the stature of hero or villain. Brutus and Cassius kill the man Caesar and not his spirit, not what he stands for, what they aim to destroy; it is a treacherous and dishonorable act which brings disorder, loss of the liberty they had sought, and finally civil war. All they had hoped to gain they lose, until they have nothing left but their names, and the opportunity to die bravely, to find freedom in suicide;

> I will proclaim my name about the field. (V, iv, 3)

Only by their deaths do they set at rest the spirit, the name of Caesar which they had sought to destroy. Their personal action is completed in this way, a tale of frustration and disorder which spreads outwards to involve the mob, the whole nation in civil destruction. All is the result of a self-deception, an obsession with names and an ignorance of reality, that could lead Brutus to think he was acting honorably in slaying his "best lover" (III, ii, 49), and Cassius to think the death of one man would bring freedom.

Julius Caesar as a Problem Play

by Ernest Schanzer

Throughout the first half of the play, then, we are given a series of images of Caesar, none of which bear much mutual resemblance, though some of them are not irreconcilable. But doubt is thrown in one way or another on the validity of most of them. And to these Shakespeare adds his own presentation of Caesar, a presentation so enigmatic and unrevealing that none of the other images are really dispelled by it. It is a dramatic treatment of Caesar in the manner of Pirandello. "Which of all these is the real Caesar?," Shakespeare seems to ask. And he takes care not to provide an answer. But does not Shakespeare further anticipate Pirandello by making us feel that perhaps there *is* no real Caesar, that he merely exists as a set of images in other men's minds and his own? For his Caesar is continuously engaged in what Pirandello calls *costruirsi,* "building himself up," creating his own image of himself, until we are left to wonder whether a lifting of the mask would reveal any face at all.

In a sense, all that Shakespeare does is to dramatize the views of Caesar and the conspirators which he found in his "sources," and especially Plutarch, distributing what are the divided and contradictory responses of a single writer among several characters who take different sides, so that what is a mental conflict in Plutarch and others becomes a dramatic conflict in his play (Brutus alone exhibits a divided response to Caesar). Except for the much greater variety of views and the more enigmatic portrayal of Caesar himself, Shakespeare's procedure is not so very different from that found in *Cornélie* and *Caesar's Revenge.* What seems fundamentally different is the use to which this procedure is put by Shakespeare. So far from creating a fortuitous medley of attitudes to the Caesar story through the process

---

"Julius Caesar *as a Problem Play." From* The Problem Plays of Shakespeare *by Ernest Schanzer (London: Routledge & Kegan Paul Ltd., 1963), pp. 32–35. Reprinted by permission of Routledge & Kegan Paul Ltd. and Schocken Books Inc.*

of drawing on a number of divergent sources (as would seem to be the case with *Caesar's Revenge*), or merely endowing Caesar with certain characteristics in order to satisfy the anticipations of Elizabethan playgoers, as H. M. Ayres suggested,[1] Shakespeare seems to me to be playing on his audience's varied and divided views of Caesar, encouraging and discouraging in turn each man's preconceptions. And since on our view of Caesar depends, very largely, our judgement of the justifiability of the entire conspiracy, the whole drama is thus kept within the area of the problem play. For though, as it seems to me, Shakespeare makes abundantly clear the folly and the catastrophic consequences of the murder, he does not, I think, make clear its moral indefensibility. His enigmatic presentation of Caesar's character and motives allows responses like that of Dover Wilson to be formed. And I see no reason to doubt that there were people who shared these responses in Shakespeare's audience. In fact, the diversity of critical opinion on the main characters and on Shakespeare's attitude to the conspiracy[2] bears witness to his success in making *Julius Caesar* a problem play. It is a problem play in much the same way as Ibsen's *Wild Duck,* which has a very similar theme: the tragic mischief created by the actions of a young idealist in fulfilment of the highest principles,

[1] His argument . . . that Shakespeare turned his Caesar into the vainglorious, hubristic figure of the French Senecan Caesar-plays, because that was what Elizabethan playgoers had come to expect, seems to me to have little foundation. Even if one were to accept this view of Shakespeare as a purveyor of the expected, we simply do not know what the stage-Caesar in the public theatres before Shakespeare's play was like. The French Senecan Caesar-plays and their imitations, like Pescetti's *Cesare,* were severely academic, and even *Caesar's Revenge,* written in the much more popular manner of Marlowe and Kyd, probably never reached the public stage, for on its title-page it is stated to have been "Priuately acted by the Studentes of Trinity Colledge in Oxford."

[2] Apart from the diametrically opposed views quoted at the beginning of the chapter, almost every intermediary shade of opinion has been expressed by commentators. The *via media* is trodden by those who hold, with Kittredge, that "Shakespeare is no partisan in this tragedy. He sides neither with Caesar and his avengers nor with the party of Brutus and Cassius. The verdict, if there must be a verdict, he leaves to history" (ed. *Julius Caesar,* 1939, p. xix); and by those who claim that Shakespeare keeps our sympathy divided: e.g. by MacMillan, "The poet's aim was to produce in the first part of the play an even balance in our sympathies, so that they should waver to and fro, inclining alternately to Caesar and the conspirators" (Arden ed. of *Julius Caesar,* 1902, p. xxv); by Wilson Knight, "For the poet and the reader, like Brutus, see both sides of the question, and suffer a division of sympathy" (*The Wheel of Fire,* 1930, p. 151); and by Adrien Bonjour, "It looks indeed as if Shakespeare wanted 'to prove the moral value of suspended judgment.'" And before it is suspended, our judgment has been constantly questioned, shifted and revised; in fact, Shakespeare made of *Julius Caesar* the drama of divided sympathies. (*The Structure of "Julius Caesar,"* 1958, p. 3.)

partly through his utter blindness to what people really are like. In both cases the question is put to the audience: "Was he morally justified in doing what he did?" And in both cases the dramatist's answer seems to me to be an insistent but not a compulsive "No."

The main purpose of Shakespeare's persistent dissociation of Caesar's body and spirit is, no doubt, to show up the foolishness and futility of the assassination. The whole second part of the play is an ironic comment on Brutus's

> We all stand up against the spirit of Caesar,
> And in the spirit of men there is no blood.
> O that we then could come by Caesar's spirit,
> And not dismember Caesar! (2.1.167–70)

What is involved in the last two acts is something more than a grim pun, which makes the conspirators find that, while they have dismembered Caesar's body, his spirit, i.e. his ghost, still walks abroad, and exacts his revenge. For the spirit of Caesar is also that legendary figure, that God and Colossus, whom Cassius deplores, and whom Caesar seeks to impose upon the imagination of his countrymen. In this he is handicapped by frailties of body and character from which the murder frees him and allows the legendary Caesar to come into his own, assisted by Antony's rhetoric, just as Antony's military skill later assists that other "spirit" of Caesar, his ghost, in executing his revenge.

Guilt and Justice in Shakespeare: *Julius Caesar*

by David Daiches

Let me begin my inquiry by asking: What is guilt? If we assume that there are forces of good and of evil both at work in the world, then we might say that the guilty man is one who co-operates with the forces of evil to increase evil's effectiveness in human affairs. Innocence is on the side of the good, guilt on the side of evil. Or so it would be pleasant to believe. A closer look at life convinces us that innocence often achieves evil. If Brutus had been a less simply virtuous man, he would not have helped to kill one of his best friends and brought tyranny to Rome (the opposite of what he intended). If Othello had been less innocent, he would not have trusted Iago and so he would not have been brought to murder his wife. If Hamlet had been less of a sensitive idealist, he would not have destroyed his own house as well as the house of Polonius. A more worldly Brutus, a less morally sensitive Hamlet, a tougher and more cunning Othello, would have done less harm in the world. The first tragic problem faced by Shakespeare in his maturity concerns the ambiguity of innocence.

This problem goes far deeper than the relation between private and public virtue, which is in some degree the theme of *Julius Caesar*. It includes, among other problems, that of the relation between innocence and virtue, or at least between innocence of character and effectiveness of moral action. It is an old dilemma. Milton was to treat it, in his own way, in *Paradise Lost,* where "our credulous mother, Eve" allowed herself to be fooled by Satan into tasting of the forbidden tree. If Satan, in the form of the serpent, had been telling the truth, then Eve would have done right to believe him and to eat of the fatal fruit. Eve's real fault was lack of sophistication; she was unsuspicious of what the serpent told her; she was, to use the American

"Guilt and Justice in Shakespeare: Julius Caesar." *From* Literary Essays *by David Daiches (Chicago: The University of Chicago Press, 1956), pp. 2–5. Reprinted by permission of the publisher.*

slang term, a "sucker" and swallowed his story. But is it morally wrong to be a sucker—as Eve was with respect to the serpent, as Othello was with respect to Iago, as Brutus was with respect to such political sophisticates as Antony, as Hamlet was, we might almost say, with respect to life?

Innocence plays into the hands of evil; only the tarnished and sophisticated mind can achieve that approximate good which alone lies within human reach. Is this one of the themes of Shakespearian tragedy? Perhaps; but before we conclude that it is we must inquire a little more closely. The case of Brutus is that of the liberal intellectual in a world of *Realpolitik*—a familiar enough case in the modern world. Cassius is the co-hero of the play, and, skilled politician though he is, with little scruple in playing on Brutus's finer feelings, he admires Brutus and cannot help allowing Brutus to achieve moral ascendancy over him, once the murder of Caesar is accomplished. The coarser nature is dominated by the finer, to the destruction of both of them and of the ideal to which they had sacrificed everything. In the quarrel scene it is Cassius who first gives way, and it is under the influence of this moral domination by Brutus that, against his better judgement, Cassius allows Brutus to have his way in the ill-advised plan of seeking immediate battle at Philippi. Nowhere is the Epicurean Cassius more like the Stoic Brutus than when he commits suicide because he is ashamed of having lived "so long, to see my best friend ta'en before my face." And that suicide, rather than military defeat, seals the doom of the republican cause. But Cassius is not as unlike Brutus as he thinks he is. Though he is the shrewder and the more practical, he is basically an idealist too, an intellectual, whom Caesar had come to suspect because "he thinks too much." If he appears as a cunning man of action beside Brutus, he is almost equally a babe in the wood when seen beside Antony, the man without innocence, the man who knows how to unite his personal affections with his political ambitions. (Though Shakespeare shows us in *Antony and Cleopatra* what happens when that unstable equilibrium collapses.) In *Julius Caesar* Antony's is the success story; he is the tarnished man who knows how to come to terms with life. He is not evil—he is generous, noble and kind-hearted—but he lacks innocence: he is post-lapsarian man, who has adapted himself to life after the Fall.

Wherein lies Antony's success? Is it not in his ability to manipulate people, to act the puppeteer and utilize the worthy emotions of innocent people for his own purposes? Cassius does this in a very mild way with Brutus, but Antony is the great puppeteer of the play, and his famous oration is the work of a supreme puppet master. He manipulates other people's innocence. So does Richard III, and Edmund in *King Lear,* and Iago. But we are not to conclude from this that Antony is intended to be a villain like these characters: that would be manifestly absurd. Richard III and Edmund and Iago are evil; Antony is sophisticated and cunning, but far from evil. All four manipulate the innocence of others for their own ends. Antony stands midway between innocence and evil, the tarnished sensual man, the man whose way of life is—to use a term the politicians are now so fond of—above all *viable.* "Human nature being what it is," Antony's way is not to be rejected out of hand. But I have a friend who says that whenever he has had a guest at dinner who has begun a political conversation with the remark, "human nature being what it is," he always counts the spoons. The argument is an excuse for being content with imperfection: one could not imagine Brutus or Hamlet using it.

Antony manipulates his self-interest and his ideals into a compromise that is above all practicable. He is too good to be a tragic villain, too bad to be a tragic hero. Are we to say, then, that he is Shakespeare's ideal practical man? Shakespeare answers that question for us in his *Antony and Cleopatra,* which shows us, as Granville-Barker has said, the nemesis of the sensual man. The unstable equilibrium cannot last; Antony in the end surrenders wholly to his passions and loses the political world to young Octavius Caesar, the man whose fortunes he had earlier saved. *There,* perhaps, is Shakespeare's ideal practical man, Octavius Caesar, shrewd, cool-headed, altogether a cold fish. Obviously it is not the ideal practical man who is the glory of the human species, and we do not need Octavius to tell us that practical success was not, for Shakespeare, the greatest thing in life.

The Images of Caesar

by Maurice Charney

In a very direct sense the "image" of a dramatic character is the actor performing the role in the theater. It is his task to embody in his person the imagery of the text and to present this realization to the audience. This is the mimetic, presentational core of the drama. In the role of Caesar, for example, the crucial contrast between the great public figure and the infirm private man—or what Knights calls "the person and the public persona, the face and the mask"—is largely a matter of acting and stage presentation. The contrast is certainly developed verbally, but the most effective image of Caesar's double nature is the one we receive from the actor in the theater.

Critics of *Julius Caesar* have been inclined to make strong and final judgments of the character of Caesar. Brandes calls him "a miserable caricature" and thinks "It was because of Shakespeare's lack of historical and classical culture that the incomparable grandeur of the figure of Caesar left him unmoved." Schücking, however, believes it "quite absurd to suppose that Shakespeare diminishes the importance of Caesar. Rather must we say that *the vastness of his figure is tacitly or openly presupposed in all the happenings of the play.*" The truth about the paradoxical figure of Caesar cannot be resolved at either extreme, and his real character and intentions were debatable even in antiquity. The official Caesar of Shakespeare's play is presented with all the pomp and ceremony of a great public person. Yet he is curiously undercut by our image of Caesar the private man, full of physical infirmities and an irritating insistence on his own dignity. Dowden puts the matter very well when he observes that Caesar has become

---

"The Images of Caesar." From Shakespeare's Roman Plays *by Maurice Charney (Cambridge, Mass.: Harvard University Press, 1961), pp. 66–70.*

to himself legendary and mythical. The real man Caesar disappears for himself under the greatness of the Caesar myth. He forgets himself as he actually is, and knows only the vast legendary power named Caesar. He is a *numen* to himself, speaking of Caesar in the third person, as if of some power above and behind his consciousness.

The people love the public spectacle of Caesar and their acclamations tend to deify him. In the first scene of the play they have come out to welcome him home after his victory over Pompey's sons in Spain, "and to rejoice in his triumph" (I, i, 36). They look upon this ceremony as a public entertainment or play with Caesar as protagonist; for, as Casca tells us,

> If the tag-rag people did not clap him and hiss him, according as he pleas'd and displeas'd them, as they use to do the players in the theatre, I am no true man. (I, ii, 260–63)

This ominous image of the people as audience, essentially fickle and easily moved as Antony's oration shows us so conclusively, also underlies the interview of Brutus and Cassius in I, ii. Although we do not actually see the mob, we are kept aware of its dealings with Caesar in the market place by off-stage sounds: *"Flourish and shout"* (I, ii, 78 s.d.) and *"Shout. Flourish"* (I, ii, 131 s.d.). Both of these occasions are marked by Brutus' apprehensive comments: "What means this shouting? I do fear the people/Choose Caesar for their king" (I, ii, 79–80); and afterward:

> Another general shout?
> I do believe that these applauses are
> For some new honours that are heap'd on Caesar.
> (I, ii, 132–34)

These shouts and flourishes are a good example of presentational images that are not visual. We do not see the people, but the noise we hear presents an image of them—an ambiguous one, too, which increases the tension of Cassius' effort to persuade Brutus and serves as an ironic commentary on it. These sound-effects images are linked with the verbal imagery by Brutus' comments.

That the people want a Caesar is most graphically illustrated by their reaction to Brutus' funeral oration. "Let him be Caesar" (III, ii, 56), shouts the Third Plebeian, and the Fourth continues in the same spirit: "Caesar's better parts/ Shall be crown'd in Brutus" (III, ii, 56–57). The mob needs a Caesar, and now that Julius is dead, his assassin can easily supply the office. And he will be given the full imperial ceremony of a "triumph home unto his house" (III, ii, 54) and "a statue with his ancestors" (III, ii, 55). The mob is not concerned with Caesar the man, but only with Caesar as a public image. These exclamations also at once deny the whole political issue of the conspiracy.

The strongest images of Caesar's imperial splendor occur when he first appears in I, ii. His impressiveness here is emphasized by the staging. He is carried in a litter above the heads of all present, clearly set apart from his followers and from the crowd that has come to see him—and the crowd needs to be large enough to serve as a tribute to Caesar's magnificence. At the outset we observe that his power to command is instantaneous. His "Calphurnia" brings Casca's immediate "Peace, ho! Caesar speaks" (I, ii, 1). The music ceases at once and there is a general hush which isolates Caesar's words and directs attention to them. This ceremony is repeated when the Soothsayer calls "Caesar!" (I, ii, 12) from the crowd:

> *Caes.* Ha! Who calls?
> *Casca.* Bid every noise be still. Peace yet again!
> (I, ii, 13–14)

Again the music ceases and Caesar addresses the Soothsayer in the imperial third person: "Speak. Caesar is turn'd to hear" (I, ii, 17). He then dismisses the Soothsayer and departs with an impressive line of imperatives: "He is a dreamer. Let us leave him. Pass" (I, ii, 24). In these twenty-four lines of I, ii we have all the essential characteristics of the official Caesar. He is strongly distinguished from his followers and from the Roman mob by his physical appearance, his style of speech, and the attitude of deference in those around him.

In this scene, too, we have the magical use of the name "Caesar" that becomes significant later on. Granville-Barker observes that "We hear the name sounded—sounded rather than spoken—seven times in twenty-four lines." The use of the third person, "Caesar," rather than the first person pronoun tends to merge Caesar the man with Caesar the political figure. This identification is one of the sources of the pride that leads to Caesar's murder, for by mingling the personal with the public, Caesar claims for himself as a man the greatness and objective power of a political function.

Julius Caesar and the King's Language

by Sigurd Burckhardt

My aim in what follows is to interpret seven of Shakespeare's plays in a way that will reveal an inner logic in the development of his dramatic poetry. I do not find this logic in archetypal myths nor in conceptual antinomies such as appearance and reality or will and reason; I find it in what, for the poet, is a stubbornly concrete substance: language. As I read them, the plays testify to Shakespeare's gradual, and painful, discovery of his medium and thereby of his own true function and powers.

I must begin with some cursory remarks about that most slippery of words: truth. The condition a statement has to meet to be called true is commonly conceived to be simple: a true statement is one which corresponds to the matter of fact it purports to describe. But truth is, of course, much more complex than this. There is, for example, the automatically true statement, which institutes or creates the corresponding matter of fact—as when a sovereign declares his country to be at war with another. The trouble with statements of this sort is that, being automatically true, they are not really true at all; where the possibility of error or falsehood is ruled out *a priori,* truth has no meaning. A second kind of statement which shows that truth is no simple one-to-one relation is the equivocation. Iseult's oath of fidelity, made good by God though it was, was not a truth, since it was meant to be misinterpreted by her listeners. (And in the end God sees to it that the balance is righted: though Iseult has, by equivocation, saved her pretty hands from burning, she loses lover and life by the black-for-white lie of her namesake, Iseult of the White Hands.) Truth, then, is at least a three-way relation, a correspondence of fact, state-

"Julius Caesar *and the King's Language." From "The King's Language: Shakespeare's Drama as Social Discovery" by Sigurd Burckhardt,* Antioch Review, *XXI (1961), 369–71, 374–79. Reprinted by permission of Mrs. Peggy Burckhardt.*

ment, and understanding. It takes two to tell the truth as well as to quarrel; truth has a social dimension.

A poet may, of course, claim to speak creatively, to give an airy nothing a local habitation and a name. But since he lacks the authority which alone can give this claim objective force, his airy nothings remain in or, after their brief hour upon the stage, revert to their original state: breath, a slight commotion of the air, is all they are. This is all right as long as the poet is satisfied with being an entertainer; the applause of his audience vindicates his enterprise. But—a good deal of "hard-boiled" Shakespeare criticism notwithstanding—Shakespeare was more ambitious; the man who wrote, "The play's the thing wherein I'll catch the conscience of the King," and who claimed for his magic that it enabled "all of us to find ourselves when no man was his own," had grander designs.

But if the poet ascends, or descends, to the level of ordinary speech and subjects himself to the normal criteria of truth, he encounters other difficulties. Modern criticism has made us wary of considering even a lyric poem the direct, personal utterance of the poet; poems have been described as verbal icons and hypothetical verbal structures; they have even been called "mute," "dumb," and "wordless." A play is clearly no direct utterance; we have no warrant to accept anything said in it as the poet's personal communication to us. It may be considered—as it often has been—a replica of life; but the imitation theory leads to endless difficulties, especially with Shakespeare; and again there is ample reason to think that Shakespeare himself did not subscribe to it. In what sense, then, can a poem be true? That is to say, what matter of fact does it state in such a way that purport and understanding coincide? I hope to show that for Shakespeare the matter of fact to which poetry must be true, and through which it and the poet remain indissolubly tied to the social order, is language itself.

In every dialogue the social order is a silent but essential partner; the simplest remark presupposes two analogously structured habit systems, and consequently the faith that the social order is coherent and pervasive enough to have instilled the same habits in the listener as in the speaker. In a radical sense, therefore, all speech is question-begging: it presupposes the community which it pretends to establish. One can imagine a social order so fully and rigorously articulated that language atrophies into a mere system of vocal signals (armies tend toward being such orders); on the other hand, where the social order has its boundaries, linguistic boundaries will develop which in time will become barriers, while within the order itself the need for a standard language is felt as strongly as that for a standard currency.

The fact that the social order acts as the ultimate mediator and therefore is directly involved in the speaking of truth (in the tri-cornered sense I have defined) has grave implications. For there can then be no truth without it, and yet the order itself may be a perversion. Or again, as long as truth and justice simply echo each other, with no possibility of recourse from one to the other, they may become a perfect but empty tautology, compelled to deny legitimate human aspirations, because to admit them would endanger the order's stability. Finally, if the order disintegrates, language is likely to disintegrate with it. Shakespeare's plays, in their progress, are explorations of these various possibilities and of their consequences for the poet. . . .

But *The Merchant of Venice* still rests on faith: faith in the basic justice and stability of the state. At the beginning of what is called Shakespeare's tragic period, this faith is shattered, and the poet begins to explore the desperate consequences of the state's disintegration or corruption.

Julius Caesar presents disintegration as it occurs: the daggers that rend Caesar's body rend the body politic. And language, thus deprived of its support, acts strangely and destructively. Brutus and Antony are not merely opposite characters; they use language differently. Brutus the Stoic relies on a kind of disembodied truth and on men's natural reason; he thinks it a simple matter to bring the two together, and once they are brought together, he cannot conceive of their being separated. Justice and truth, for him, do not reside in the state and in language, but beyond them, free of contingency and circumstance. He acts and speaks accordingly; with a bloodless and inhuman logic ("And in the spirit of men there is no blood") he dissects the living, integral man and gives each separate part its separate due: "As Caesar loved me, I weep for him; as he was fortunate, I rejoice at it; as he was valiant, I honour him; but, as he was ambitious, I slew him."

Antony's deadliness is of a different sort; it is bloodily corporeal. To him the death of Caesar means no return to a more natural order, but chaos with its horror and its opportunity. He makes himself the very voice of Caesar's gashes:

> Over thy wounds now do I prophesy,
> Which, like dumb mouths, do ope their ruby lips

> To beg the voice and utterance of my tongue. . . .
> Domestic fury and fierce civil strife
> Shall cumber all the parts of Italy.

Truth and justice have become empty sounds; language, like the money of Caesar's legacy, is now merely a means, to be seized and used by the strongest.

The recoil upon the poet is immediate. Two poets appear in the play, in two brief and seemingly inconsequential scenes. Cinna, who has the ill fortune to be namesake to one of Caesar's murderers, is halted by a mob and lynched. Vainly he protests: "I am Cinna the poet, I am Cinna the poet!" The reply is brutal and to the purpose: "It is no matter, his name's Cinna. Pluck but his name out of his heart, and turn him going." This is not only the bloody stupidity of the rabble but, in the most literal sense, poetic justice. With the social order no longer there to mediate, language deteriorates into the disembodied and the crudely physical: the realm in which words have no substance, so that they readily join in repellent conjunctions ("I, that did love Caesar when I struck him"), and the realm where words are mere physical substance, so that Cinna is Cinna, and there's an end. The poet, who, relying on the stability of the order, has played his games with language, now is killed by a pun.

The other, nameless poet is not killed; he is brushed aside as a futile prattler. He breaks into the tent where Brutus and Cassius have just composed their quarrel and admonishes them, in hackneyed rhymes, to be friends. For Shakespeare, the time is past when poets could claim a public function by rhyming political commonplaces into Mirrors for Magistrates and Schools of Princes; as Brutus says: "I'll know his humour when he knows his time. What should the wars do with these jiggling fools?" Long before this, Shakespeare had discovered a profounder and truer function for poetry; if we recall how Portia became its embodiment in the social order of Venice, we will not miss the more than merely personal weight of Brutus' "Portia's dead." It is a different Portia, to be sure, but so was Cinna a different Cinna and yet was killed. For Shakespeare, it's not in dreams but in names that responsibilities begin.

In *Hamlet* the body politic is corrupted more slowly and insidiously, by poison—administered through the *ear*. What we see in the play is the gradual working of this poison—most directly on Hamlet's mind, but through it on the entire court, innocent and guilty alike, until in the final scene it breaks into open virulence on the point of swords.

And the pollution of the order presents itself to Hamlet in the form not merely of murder, but of incest. To apply the terms of my interpretation: in a perverted order the union of language and authority is incestuous, one lying (in the punning senses of the word) with the other in an unholy embrace. The discovery that this is so is both paralyzing and dangerous to the poet.

The paralysis of Hamlet's will is the most famous crux in criticism. A generation ago it led T. S. Eliot to formulate the doctrine of the objective correlative; he saw the crux as evidence of Shakespeare's inability to find an adequate embodiment for Hamlet's (and also his own) emotions. But it strikes me as improbable that a play which has engaged audiences and readers so fully and for so long a time as *Hamlet* has should have, for its mainspring, a flagging of poetic invention. It seems more plausible to think of the paralysis as the consequence of a new awareness; with Eliot, Hamlet might have said: "After such knowledge, what forgiveness?"

I believe we ought to be more puzzled than critics usually have been by Hamlet's failure, or refusal, to see the murder of Claudius as a political act. The question of succession, which is implicitly at issue, is the most important political question in monarchies, and Shakespeare himself had so treated it many times over. Claudius speaks of Hamlet as the heir apparent, as do Laertes and Polonius; but Hamlet fixes with seemingly obstinate blindness upon the purely private aspects of the revenge. In this he stands in sharp contrast to both Laertes and Fortinbras; the former particularly does not hesitate to make his private quarrel a public cause. Not once does Hamlet, in his self-searching and self-admonitions, try to draw resolution from the manifest truth that Denmark is ruled by a criminal usurper, and that he himself is not only a man personally wronged but also the legitimate heir, to whose succession the wronged state has as much right as he himself.

Eliot may well be right in surmising that "Hamlet's bafflement . . . is a prolongation of the bafflement of his creator in the face of his artistic problem." My only *caveat* would be against the word "artistic." The poet has moved close to the center of sovereignty and shrinks back in disgust and fear, because language—by which and through which he must exercise this sovereignty—is incestuously tied to the corrupt order and thus involves him in its corruption. His ideal function—the standing surety to those immediate personal unions through which the order is continually regenerated—is no longer fulfillable;

his voice is now necessarily a public one, as Laertes explains to Ophelia:

> He may not, as unvalued persons do,
> Carve for himself, for on his choice depends
> The sanity and health of the whole state;
> And therefore must his choice be circumscrib'd
> Unto the voice and yielding of that body
> Whereof he is the head. Then, if he says he loves you,
> It fits your wisdom so far to believe it
> As he in his particular act and phrase
> May give his saying deed; which is no further
> Than the main voice of Denmark goes withal.

But the main voice of Denmark being Claudius', speech for Hamlet is almost always divisive; words are beaten into swords. They are hooks to catch the conscience of the king, daggers to enter the queen's ear. They are ineffectual in prayer but of marvellous force in cursing; even in self-communion and toward Ophelia they are all edge: "You are keen, my lord, you are keen." One of the oddest passages in the play is Hamlet's answer to Gertrude's contrite question: "What shall I do?" (III, iv) "Not this, by no means, that I bid you do," he replies and then, in loathsome detail, bids her betray his secret to the king. Why the elaborate double negative? Because language draws its force and urgency from the representation of what is sordid, "rank," "stew'd in corruption"; so that good is a negation of evil, rather than evil a deficiency of good. "Custom" has this potential of negative goodness; though it is "damned" and "monstrous," though it transforms drunkard Danes into beasts and hardens grave-diggers into insensibility (elsewhere in Shakespeare, "customer" means "whore"), yet

> That monster custom, who all sense doth eat
> Of habits evil, is angel yet in this,
> That to the use of actions fair and good
> He likewise gives a frock and livery,
> That aptly is put on.

Despairing, therefore, of the very possibility of love and truth, Hamlet bids Ophelia go into the nunnery—meaning either a convent or a brothel—into a purity that is merely sterile or into a vile and venal promiscuity. (Isabella, heroine of the later *Measure for Measure,* has followed Hamlet's command; she has opted for untainted sterility, but is forced to expose herself to the threat of having to sell herself. Her dilemma is resolved by the machinations of the absconded sovereign, who works behind the scenes, truly a playwright, to bring about a somewhat *ad hoc* happy ending.) Hamlet's "I say, we will have no more marriages" is programmatic for Shakespeare's tragic period; the true fulfilment of his craft—the "marriage of true minds," which he had celebrated and embodied in the great romantic comedies—will not be granted him and us again until *Antony and Cleopatra.*

I see, then, in *Hamlet,* not so much the bafflement of the poet who cannot find an adequate embodiment for his feelings, but rather the shrinking from the knowledge he has gained. How is he to wrest truth from a medium which has no being apart from the social order and is by this very order corrupted to falsehood? How, in other words, is he to get rid of the third partner to every dialogue, when that partner stands revealed as an ear-poisoner? There are two possible ways, both explored by Shakespeare and both fraught with tragedy: the faith that language, in and by itself, *is* a true medium, at least in the poet's hands; or, conversely, that the poet can speak as an absolute sovereign, who, by virtue of this creative sovereignty, endows speech with the *a priori* truth it must have if he is not to be a liar and accomplice to corruption. *Othello* and *King Lear* explore these alternatives.

To Know Himself: An Aspect of Tragic Structure

by Robert B. Heilman

To know a man well were to know himself. *Hamlet*

In point of years Shakespeare was at least half-way through his career as writer of tragedy before he began to think seriously of the tragic hero as a figure capable of self-awareness and self-judgment. In the earlier tragedies, his way of conceiving the dramatic situation tended to block the emergence of self-understanding in the hero. A long and bitter feud does not lead naturally to the confrontation of self, for the participants are immersed in the confrontation of enemies. In a feud—as in a duel, which is a feud *in petto*—all energy goes into attack and survival; simply to carry on, one must withhold all self-estimates; one's working assumption is self-approbation.

Titus Andronicus, Romeo and Juliet, and *Julius Caesar* are rooted in feuds or in civil likenesses of them. In *Titus,* of course, the reciprocal acts of revenge become parodistic, the frantic exacerbation of melodramatic appeal a caricature. Still the bloody theatricality manages to embody, expressionistically, a frenzied maliciousness not wholly incomprehensible to us. A moral epidemic, we know, may ravage a community. In Aaron a measure of the naturalistic—he becomes understandable as an "outsider" and as a father—undergirds a role that is primarily symbolic: he incorporates an ultimate resentment that craves only to humiliate and destroy. He is the only character who has a sense of self, and he records a perversity that, for all of its self-conscious theatricalism, does not falsify the portrait: "If one good deed in all my life I did, I do repent it from my very soul" (V, iii,

"To Know Himself: An Aspect of Tragic Structure" by Robert B. Heilman. From A Review of English Literature, *V (April, 1964), 36–43. Reprinted by permission of the author and* A Review of English Literature.

189–90).[1] If other elements in the play are unconscious parodies by excess, this speech is self-conscious parody by reversal: the reversal of the tragic recognition that Shakespeare was to labour toward for some years.

A duel is the assertion of the self as it is. It is an uncriticized "I" against "them." Whatever its role in exacting a kind of accountability or in testing the fear of shame or the timbre of one's own moral assurance, nevertheless it is open to indiscriminate use by anyone, though his merits as challenger for a cause may be hopelessly outweighed by his homicidal inclinations. The duel, then, provides a stylized public outlet for private impulses to injure or destroy, or even strengthens them by furnishing them an exercise otherwise inhibited by the social order. To the Capulets Tybalt was evidently a charming fellow, but as voice of the feud he is only strident and insolent. In this context it is remarkable that Shakespeare should have imagined Romeo as being, in any way or at any time, other than the thoughtless upholder of the Montague position. Yet Romeo the lover does try to placate the abusive Tybalt: he opposes another value to the imperatives of the "ancient quarrel." He does this, we may say, instinctively. Years later, the rival claims of love and hate might have established themselves in the protagonist's consciousness and thus set up a drama of self-confrontation not unlike Macbeth's. This does not happen in *Romeo and Juliet:* Romeo's surges of feeling are never polarized about incompatible claims that he must anguish over. Though he is pushed about by antithetical forces, he does not wrestle with them, choose one, and then chide himself for neglecting the other. Or rather, he goes through this course only once, after he has refused to strike back at Tybalt and has seen Mercutio fatally wounded, who,

> My very friend, hath got this mortal hurt
> In my behalf, my reputation stained
> With Tybalt's slander. (III, i, 109–11)

He censures himself for having tried to keep the peace; it is a self-judgment by a very conventional standard, and, compared with Gloucester's and Lear's self-indictments for errors of commission, it notes only a failure to commit violence. Romeo then makes the conventional response to Tybalt's renewed challenge.

[1] Quotations are taken from *The Works of Shakespeare,* ed. Sir A. Quiller-Couch and J. Dover Wilson (1921). [The New Cambridge edn.]

After killing Tybalt he once again takes a momentary look at himself. Does not Juliet, he asks the Nurse,

> . . . think me an old murderer,
> Now I have stained the childhood of our joy
> With blood removed but little from her own? (III, iii, 95–97)

And he refers to the "cursed hand" that "Murdered her kinsman" (103–4). This is not simply rhetorical, of course, but the implicit self-reproach is in a given context: the mirror is less conscience than it is Juliet, and the felt wrongdoing is less "I have committed a murder" than it is, "I have brought death to her kinsman" and "stain'd . . . our joy." The hero's sense of things is less "I am a moral agent" than it is "I am encountering a harsh ironic fate."

There is, then, not much drama of self-awareness; the tension derives rather from the conflict of desire and circumstance. That is, for the most part, the mode of the play: the direction of consciousness outward, away from the self toward problems shaped by the world. *Vis-à-vis* Rosaline, Romeo is the conventional heavy lover, a bit sorry for himself, reading "mine own fortune in my misery" (I, ii, 59); enter Juliet, and he instantly concludes that he "ne'er saw true beauty till this night" (I, v, 53). The redirection of passion does not pose a problem for his consciousness; this is, of course, not to say that it should, but simply to notice where the drama takes its stand. When Friar Laurence, who had wanted to slow down the Rosaline affair, is astonished to find that it has come to a dead stop, Romeo says only "I have forgot that name, and that name's woe" (II, iii, 46) and censures Rosaline for not reciprocating as Juliet does.

For him, the instinctive structuring of experience is himself against persons or forces that can be blamed—Rosaline or fortune: "O, I am fortune's fool!" (III, i, 136). Learning of Tybalt's death, Juliet is more double-minded; she has to struggle through conflicting emotions while keenly aware of each; the fourteen-year-old is more mature than her older lover. News of banishment drives Romeo into a single-track outbreak close to tantrums; he grovels "on the ground, with his own tears made drunk" (III, iii, 85), and he makes his first try at suicide, in quick despair like sad young men in Chekhov and Ibsen. Then, after the long pressure on Juliet, the drug plot, and the protracted scenes of "death" and mourning, Romeo in Mantua gets a false report and without delay resolves again on death. In the fifty-line soliloquy before he takes his drug, he speaks for three lines of paying a debt to Tybalt by taking his own life; but this incidental generosity of a dying man does not materially alter the dominant note of "inauspicious stars" and "world-wearied flesh," that is, of inimical forces that have sapped the will to live.

This world is one of accidents, automatic combat, and some scheming; these cut down a great erotic passion. Here that passion is the only felt imperative, in contrast with *Antony and Cleopatra,* where rival imperatives must trouble consciousness. *Romeo and Juliet* offers little arena for the moral struggles that emerge when the protagonist must face himself, that is, the contradictions in the nature of the full self. To say this is simply to distinguish, within the broad realm of tragedy, between the dramas of lesser range and greater range, those in which the most serious delinquencies and aggressions reveal the full self and have to be understood and morally placed. An old, rather popular term for *Romeo and Juliet,* "tragedy of young love," happens to suggest the absence of full maturity in the hero or, to change the perspective, that the author had not yet come to a deep exploration of personality. Romeo evokes sympathy that contains, as an accompaniment of its ease, a measure of unwitting condescension. Yet in the imagery there is a pressure of thought which partly compensates for the lack of human amplitude: the persistent love-death theme pushes beyond the grief of unfulfilment to metaphysicalize the simple adversities of circumstance.

To move from *Romeo and Juliet* to *Julius Caesar* is to change worlds; the two plays themselves provide the distinguishing terms. The first is the world of "star-cross'd" protagonists; in the second, "The fault . . . is not in our stars, But in ourselves" (*Julius Caesar,* I, ii, 140–41). The first is one of "unreasonable" Romeo (III, iii, 111); the second is that of Caesar, whose "affections [never] swayed More than his reason" (II, i, 20–21), of Cassius, who "thinks too much" (I, ii, 195), and of political competitors whose always active ratiocinative talents, primarily at the operational but also at the theoretical level, make this the first of the tragedies in which intellect is conspicuously present. While Brutus articulates the ends and the style of political action, Cassius and Antony reveal a brilliant grasp of the structure of both personalities and situations. Among three or four characters there is so much awareness of the strengths and vulnerabilities of others, and of the ways in which others must be approached to secure desired responses, that there is a constant air of intellectual melodrama; it is not stupid people who engage in various rhetorical sorties and campaigns. In one way or another there is enough mind at work to let us suppose that one of the objects of mind will be the self. Consciousness implies self-consciousness. Yet in *Julius Caesar* it is rare that anyone holds a mirror to the self. Portia makes some self-analytical remarks (in II, i, to Brutus, and in II, iv, to herself, in the presence of Lucius), but these are static observations, a part of the domestic garnishing of the main political dish; no moral action hinges on them.

We are driven back to the feud and its restricting of awareness to action against the foe and counter-action, for *Julius Caesar* is dominated by what Antony calls "Domestic fury and fierce civil strife" (III, i, 264). Yet civil broils are not necessarily incompatible with the drama of the soul, however much they may tend to confine and minimize it. In *Lear, Macbeth, Antony and Cleopatra,* and *Coriolanus* there are overwhelming civil broils, and yet the drama is fundamentally within the protagonists; the dramatic structuring of experience is quite different from that of *Julius Caesar.* It took Shakespeare some time to learn the kind of dramatic orientation that first appears fully in *Lear*: in the later tragedies, the commotion within the state is secondary to the turmoil within the individual, to actions that have been taken in answer to some personal need or passion. In *Romeo and Juliet* and in *Julius Caesar,* on the contrary, the antecedent fact is the public situation—the feud or the apparent development of a political dictatorship—and we see the private life in this context. The private life is result rather than cause, or response rather than stimulus; whatever intensity and individuality of feeling may drive the characters, the perspective is, in modern parlance, sociological. Not until *Coriolanus* did Shakespeare reach the point at which he could take off from the political or social context, move from that to the individual psyche, and then let the latter assume dramatic primacy. (This is not to beg the question of where *Coriolanus* belongs in the artistic hierarchy of the plays.) He certainly moved in this direction in *Hamlet,* where, almost without warning or precedent in his own work, he produced a highly self-conscious hero; in *Hamlet,* however, there is the problem of the relationship between self-consciousness and self-knowledge, to which we come shortly. Suddenly in *Othello* Shakespeare shifted to the inner life as the genesis of drama; only in a minor way, however, did he here follow through into public life those repercussions of private decisions that were to assume such magnitude in *Lear* and *Macbeth* and to endow these plays with their exceptional moral comprehensiveness. This large measuring of public consequences, what is more, accompanies the most rigorous exploration of consciousness and of the painful divisions within it—a probing of self-knowledge that reaches one kind of peak in Macbeth's "Twere best not know myself."

From that we are still a long way off in *Julius Caesar,* in which the protagonists, far from fleeing and renouncing self-knowledge, have hardly crossed within its borders. Either Shakespeare is not yet ready for such portraiture, or he rejects it. What draws one's eye here is that he conceives of Cassius and Brutus in ways that might lead to a drama of consciousness: he presents both as having actual or potential divisions that are the raw material of self-confrontation and self-knowledge. Cassius is both a plotter and a born follower; his raw unprotected ego, his sensitiveness to slight, and his political idealism are not always clearly distinguishable; his shrewdness of perception is not matched by his force in execution; his need for love and his capacity for resentment can drive him, under frustrating conditions, close to hysteria. Here, in a man of no mean intelligence, are matters for pondering and understanding. Yet Cassius asks questions only of Brutus (IV, iii), not of himself; he accounts for his disturbed state by blaming heredity; he appears to have no doubts about the colour of his political motives; and with Romeo's haste and Romeo's hasty conclusion, based like Romeo's on misinformation, he arranges death for himself. Consciousness is destroyed without ever having opened itself to some of its most suitable materials. Cassius's "Caesar, thou art revenged" (V, iii, 46) is hardly a self-judgement; it is rather an ironic observation reversing the "he who laughs last" truism.

Brutus is an idealist who has to get dirty hands; he knows that he and the others in the coup "appear bloody and cruel" (III, i, 166), but he hopes to save reality against this appearance; his wife detects "some sick offence within your mind" (II, i, 268), and even he acknowledges a "sad heart" (290). Out of this might grow some self-interrogation, some wondering, especially in a man by no means thoughtless. But Shakespeare has chosen to show him as a man of narrower range, with a singular closure against alternative views, and not to criticize that narrowness by making dramatic capital of its inadequacy either as a moral fact or as a guide to practical politics. In Brutus he finds a self-assurance that either proscribes self-questioning or assumes that all answers are known. It is a remarkable case of *hubris,* in the realms of both tactics and motives, not brought to book;

the play does not really develop the irony that, with slight changes in the characters, the revolt might have worked; much less makes the characters, Brutus above all, realize this fact and find in it a mirror of self. Brutus's defeat and his nobility are presented neutrally as facts, and the latter is permitted to embrace conscious rectitude—without its becoming, as it would in a later age, a trap. Whereas our condescension to Romeo is unconscious, since we share in his erotic triumph, our condescension to Brutus is overt, since we cannot share in his moral and administrative complacency. In the present context the point is that Brutus is not given full development as a tragic character; Shakespeare, we surmise, has not yet reached the point at which he can see character as complexly as he was to see it in Lear and Macbeth.

A reader reluctant to question the dramatist's sensibility might argue that Shakespeare's imagination was insubordinate at a few points and undercut his formal acceptance of Brutus by letting Brutus's humourless self-content become evident enough to constitute a judgement on him. It is a possible view, but it is rendered improbable by the vigour with which Shakespeare works in the opposite direction. He gives the emphatic concluding lines of the play to Antony's "noblest Roman" speech and Octavius's assent to it. In taking over from Plutarch the apparition of Caesar's ghost to Brutus, Shakespeare flattens the business out into an almost lifeless formality of revenge. The visitation meant, in North's words, "that the gods were offended with the murther of Caesar"—an open invitation to introduce, in Brutus, an inquiry into deed and self. Compare the appearance of Banquo's ghost to Macbeth, in whom the intense inner pressures here come to the surface. In *Julius Caesar* there is nothing of the kind; Brutus, though he knows he will not win, still retains inner peace. His suicide has no trace of that self-judgement, incomplete though it may be, that precedes Othello's. Shakespeare's imagination is not yet carrying him into the inner puzzles of tragic character.

Julius Caesar and Plutarch

by Geoffrey Bullough

In action *Julius Caesar* is a tragic chronicle with three main foci: the seduction of Brutus; the assassination and its concomitants; and the vengeance of Antony in which his rise and Octavius' are contrasted with the decline and fall of Brutus and Cassius. The foregoing analysis shows that Shakespeare drew freely throughout on Plutarch's three *Lives*. Probably the fact that he had three biographies before him suggested a threefold division in which first Brutus was the main (though not the only) centre of interest, then Caesar, and lastly Antony with Octavius. Having to piece together the deeds and motives of the participants out of three accounts Shakespeare was encouraged not to make any of them—the noble conspirator, the world-famous victim, the dexterous avenger—into the sole hero of his play. His own interest seems to have been divided between them, and since in Plutarch and other histories none of the three was above reproach, and all were portrayed with a mixture of approval and disapproval, the paradoxes of motivation and morality seem to have seized Shakespeare's imagination and inspired or fortified his disinclination to make any one of them the central figure. Rather he prefers to give a balanced view, pointing out the mingled good and evil in their behaviour, without explicit moralizing or Senecan rant. Not for him in 1599 the diatribes of Discord and the Ghost which girdle *Caesar's Revenge*. His studies in English history had shown him how mixed was human nature both in politics and private life; and the comedies he was perhaps already writing or planning (*All's Well*, etc.) were to be darker in tone than his previous ones because in them romance was to be treated realistically in the light of deep ethical conflict.

"Julius Caesar *and Plutarch." From* Narrative and Dramatic Sources of Shakespeare *by Geoffrey Bullough (New York: Columbia University Press; London: Routledge & Kegan Paul Ltd., 1964), V, 52–57. Reprinted by permission of the publishers and the author.*

So Julius Caesar is not the "hero," although he is the pivot of the tragedy. He is the world-victor, as even Cassius bitterly admits:

> Why man, he doth bestride the narrow world
> Like a Colossus (I, ii, 133–34)

He has got "the start of the majestic world," to "bear the palm alone." He has conquered the Pompeys, and Shakespeare could depend on his audience to have the right initial awe of Caesar's greatness. In order not to make his personality dominate the play Shakespeare must play him down, and without destroying his legend reveal him not as godlike but as a man subject to other men's weaknesses.

Here we touch on one of Shakespeare's major difficulties. In discussing English history he could rely on his audience's knowing a good deal about the events of the past 250 years, for the reigns of the kings since Edward III were associated with heroic or terrible events still often recalled in religious, political and imaginative writings. Most of the barons in the plays from *Henry VI* to *Henry IV* were ancestors, direct or collateral, of Elizabethan nobles, and their family legends were widely known. The great battles of the past, the exiles, usurpations, murders and intrigues which Hall, Grafton, Holinshed and others had described were common knowledge. No such acquaintance with the details of Roman history could be assumed among the citizens who came to see Julius Caesar killed in the Capitol. Shakespeare himself could not have extracted from Plutarch or Appian or other authorities so clear an idea of the complex issues involved as was given to modern students by Mommsen, Oman and G. Walter. He seems to have wished to compose an objective and impartial picture of the interrelationship of Brutus and Cassius, Caesar, Antony and Octavius, while entering as little as possible into the complexities of the political situation. He was forced to simplify, to depart from Plutarch, not only to avoid bewildering the spectators with recondite allusions but also in order to treat the main characters with even-handed justice and divided sympathy.

To expatiate on Caesar's past exploits and the reforms which as Dictator he was planning for Rome, his acts of generosity (including his honouring of his late enemy Brutus) would be to make Brutus into the criminal Dante thought him. On the other hand, the assassination of Caesar, the strong ruler who had brought order out of chaos, must not seem a virtuous act. Shakespeare was no republican but a defender of the Tudor monarchy which had brought peace out of civil war and was always afraid of a relapse. Yet in following Plutarch's portrait of Brutus and making him a noble sinner, an altruistic murderer, the dramatist must not give tangible proof that Brutus' suspicions of Caesar's intentions were wrong.

Hence Shakespeare walks a tightrope in depicting the two chief antagonists, and succeeds by ignoring particular political issues. We do not see Caesar insulting the Senate and we are not reminded of his egoistic actions, sins against tradition, or love affairs (even Cleopatra is not mentioned); but he is viewed well on this side idolatry, and portrayed as a lover of pomp and circumstance whose tragedy is less ambition than a self-conscious arrogance not justified by the physical or mental qualities shown in the play. We see him patronizing his followers and now displaying bland indifference to warnings which we know have fatal significance, now vacillating (like any mediocre husband) between uxoriousness and public duty. Unlike Pescetti's Caesar, who is thoroughly scared and about to surround himself with an impenetrable guard, Shakespeare's Caesar perishes through a false sense of security, an assurance which misjudges the situation and the men around him. We should not believe all that the envious Cassius and Casca say against him, but some of it strikes home during the first two Acts. The balance is adjusted however by the assassination and Antony's use of it. With his death Caesar becomes a martyr, once more the Caesar of popular legend.

Similarly Brutus might easily in his crucial soliloquy (II, i) have mentioned several illboding signs of anti-republican ambition in Caesar's behavior since crossing the Rubicon. Instead Shakespeare makes him admit:

> The abuse of greatness is when it disjoins
> Remorse from power; and, to speak truth of Caesar,
> I have not known when his affections sway'd
> More than his reason (II, i, 18–21)

His decision to join the conspiracy is founded on the supposition that if crowned Caesar would change his nature ("Then lest he may, prevent"). In depriving Brutus of any substantial reason for the assassination Shakespeare distorts the historic situation, and illustrates the lack of judgment which marks Brutus' character throughout the play. His tragedy therefore is that of a man of the noblest moral principles whose idealism blinds him to the realities of politics, and to the nature of his fellow-conspirators and of the Roman populace. The good man is led to perform an act of murderous injustice. Caesar is killed undeservedly on a presupposition of what he might become; but his story is not ended with his death. "We all stand up against the spirit of Caesar," says Brutus (II, i, 167) meaning the autocratic ambition of Caesar. But the spirit of Caesar lives on in Antony and Octavius, and finally conquers. Moreover by transforming Brutus' "evil spirit" or "genius" into Caesar's ghost Shakespeare makes the Battle of Philippi a personal triumph for the dead man as well as for his avengers.

The ambivalent treatment of Caesar and Brutus is also extended to Antony. If the glory of Caesar's past made it unnecessary for Shakespeare to prove the Dictator's heroic worth in any striking fashion, so the shadow of Antony's future makes it unnecessary to expatiate on his sensual weaknesses beyond letting Caesar mention his love of plays, music and laughter (I, ii, 200–3), and showing him running the course at the Lupercal when Brutus refers to his quick, gamesome spirit (I, ii, 28–9). In this play favourable aspects of Antony are to the fore since he is to be Caesar's avenger, "a shrewd contriver" turning the tables on Brutus in the funeral scene and taking the lead in the war against the assassins. The weakness of Brutus' judgement of men is shown both in his insistence on sparing Antony's life against the advice of the more worldly-wise Cassius, and in his self-confident assurance that he could hold the people despite anything Antony, by permission, could say. Antony gains his oratorical victory in the marketplace by a dexterity which we can admire, since the conspirators have put themselves in the wrong. But the other side of his character is not forgotten. Immediately after he has stirred up the mob and given his blessing to "mischief," we see the innocent poet Cinna murdered; and in the next scene (IV, i) Antony not only takes a lead in the proscription but treats Lepidus in a contemptuous and deceitful manner which surprises Octavius. The devoted friend of Caesar proves to be moved by greed and ambition. Acts IV and V indeed press home the ambivalent treatment of the two sides, for if the mask of piety slips from the face of the avenger, the high-principled solidarity of the Republicans is seen endangered in the quarrel about bribery, money and military skill between Brutus and Cassius.

That Shakespeare wished to avoid writing just another tragedy of revenge like *The Tragedy of Pompey and Caesar* is made clear, for sympathy with Brutus and Cassius, if shaken, is not lost. Their reconciliation, manly enough in itself, is made touching by news of Portia's death, Brutus' noble grief and Cassius' warm-hearted feeling for his friend. They are gallant and loyal as they go down in defeat, and their deaths are truly Roman. On the other hand the behaviour of Antony and Octavius in their hour of victory reflects credit on them too. So the play ends in a manner which dignifies all parties in the conflict. Nobody is portrayed with total praise or total blame, but the greatest praise is given to Brutus who, despite his misguided act, is recognized to have exemplified a perfect balance of virtues: "This was a man!"

Julius Caesar is a play about a triple group-relationship—with Caesar at the centre of one group, Brutus of another, Antony of the third—and of their interaction in a great conflict which involves the fate of Rome. Unlike the French Senecans Shakespeare does not explore the political principles involved; he refers little to the horrors of the Pompeian wars (so luridly described by Lucan) and he neither prophesies the strife that followed Philippi nor treats what happens as part of a divinely-ordained movement from republic to monarchy. The play lacks the overt didacticism of the English Histories. Its emphasis is not on political theory but on the traits of individual men as shown in their public connections.

The play is not a "problem play" in the sense that we are left undecided how to regard the characters. The ambivalence of presentation is not intended to confuse or offer alternative interpretations. We are meant to accept both sides as true to life and to modulate from approval to disapproval as Plutarch himself did in his *Lives.* For what Shakespeare learned from Plutarch was to represent more clearly than before the paradoxes of human motive, the mixture of good and evil in the same person. The heroic Caesar may be pompous, deaf and epileptic; the sensual Antony may achieve nobility; the stoic Brutus be tetchy with his friend. In *Julius Caesar* the dramatist achieves a somewhat detached tolerance in his attitude towards historical figures, and at the same time a critical attitude towards politics and those who take part in it. The romantic hero-worship of *Henry V* has given place to a shrewd look at the inner weaknesses of public men. But the mood is still benevolent and the ancient world has a certain grandeur.

The Tragedy of Order: *Julius Caesar*

by Northrop Frye

In each of Shakespeare's three social tragedies, *Julius Caesar, Macbeth,* and *Hamlet,* we have a tragic action based on three main character-groups. First is the order-figure: Julius Caesar in that play; Duncan in *Macbeth*; Hamlet's father. He is killed by a rebel-figure or usurper: Brutus and the other conspirators; Macbeth; Claudius. Third comes a nemesis-figure or nemesis-group: Antony and Octavius; Malcolm and Macduff; Hamlet. It is sometimes assumed that the hero, the character with the title-role, is always at the centre of the play, and that all plays are to be related in the same way to the hero; but each of the heroes of these three tragedies belongs to a different aspect of the total action. The nemesis-figure is partly a revenger and partly an avenger. He is primarily obsessed with killing the rebel-figure, but he has a secondary function of restoring something of the previous order.

The Elizabethan social or historical tragedy shows, much more clearly than the other two kinds, the impact of heroic energy on the human condition, the wheel of fortune creaking against the greater wheel of nature. Central to the form is an Elizabethan assumption about society, which is simple but takes some historical imagination to grasp. Society to the Elizabethans was a structure of personal authority, with the ruler at its head, and a personal chain of authority extending from the ruler down. Everybody had a superior, and this fact, negatively, emphasized the limited and finite nature of the human situation. Positively, the fact that the ruler was an individual with a personality was what enabled his subjects to be individuals and to have personalities too. The man who possesses the secret and invisible virtues of human nature is the man with the quiet mind, so celebrated in Elizabethan lyric poetry. But such a man is dependent on the ceaseless vigilance of the ruler for his peace.

"The Tragedy of Order: Julius Caesar." *From* Fools of Time *by Northrop Frye (London: Oxford University Press; Toronto: University of Toronto Press, 1965), pp. 17–20, 25–27, 29–34. Reprinted by permission of the publishers.*

This view of social order, with its stress on the limited, the finite, and the individual, corresponds, as indicated above, to Nietzsche's Apollonian vision in Greek culture. That makes it hard for us to understand it. We ourselves live in a Dionysian society, with mass movements sweeping across it, leaders rising and falling, and constantly taking the risk of being dissolved into a featureless tyranny where all sense of the individual disappears. We even live on a Dionysian earth, staggering drunkenly around the sun. The treatment of the citizens in *Julius Caesar* and *Coriolanus* puzzles us: we are apt to feel that Shakespeare's attitude is anti-democratic, instead of recognizing that the situation itself is pre-democratic. In my own graduate-student days during the nineteen-thirties, there appeared an Orson Welles adaptation of *Julius Caesar* which required the hero to wear a fascist uniform and pop his eyes like Mussolini, and among students there was a good deal of discussion about whether Shakespeare's portrayal of, say, Coriolanus showed "fascist tendencies" or not. But fascism is a disease of democracy: the fascist leader is a demagogue, and a demagogue is precisely what Coriolanus is not. The demagogues in that play are the tribunes whom the people have chosen as their own managers. The people in Shakespeare constitute a "Dionysian" energy in society: that is, they represent nothing but a potentiality of response to leadership. We are apt to assume, like Brutus, that leadership and freedom threaten one another, but, for us as for Shakespeare, there is no freedom without the sense of the individual, and in the tragic vision, at least, the leader or hero is the primary and original individual. The good leader individualizes his followers; the tyrant or bad leader intensifies mass energy into a mob. Shakespeare has grasped the ambiguous nature of Dionysus in a way that Nietzsche (like D. H. Lawrence later) misses. In no period of history does Dionysus have anything to do with freedom; his function is to release us from the burden of freedom. The last thing the mob says in both *Julius Caesar* and *Coriolanus* is pure Dionysus: "Tear him to pieces."

Two contemporary plays, much simpler in their construction than any of Shakespeare's, illustrate the impact of the *facta* of fortune on the *data* of nature. At one extreme we have Marlowe's Tamburlaine, who is the Dionysian energy of fortune incarnate. Tamburlaine is a "scourge of God," conquering one demoralized society after another with nothing in the order of nature to stop him: nothing, that is, except death itself. He is a portent of the kind of limitless ferocity that would get loose if the alliance of social and natural order represented by the strong ruler were to break down. At the opposite extreme (perhaps designed to be that) we have Chapman's double play on the conspiracy and tragedy of Byron. Here the central figure is an idealized Henry IV of France, a firm, wise, patient ruler who has to deal with the excessive ambition and egotism of one of his subjects. He gives Byron every chance to fit into the social order, and only when forbearance becomes obviously impossible does he reluctantly consent to Byron's execution. One scene consists of a reported speech by Elizabeth I, and Essex is mentioned more than once in the dialogue, so it is clear that Henry IV is not the only ideal monarch in Europe. Henry and Elizabeth are what we have called order-figures, rulers whose personalities give form and shape to their kingdoms. Byron, along with Tamburlaine, is a rebel-figure: whatever his moral status he is a genuine hero, and everything about him suggests the unbounded and infinite, just as everything about the order-figure suggests law, finiteness, and the principle of individuality.

In Shakespeare's day there had been no permanently successful example of popular sovereignty. Machiavelli had drawn the conclusion that there were two forms of government: popular governments, which were unstable, and principalities, or what we should call dictatorships, the stability of which depended on the force and cunning of the prince. This analysis, of course, horrified the idealists of the sixteenth century who were trying to rationalize the government of the prince with arguments about the "general good," and so Machiavelli became, by way of the attacks on him, a conventional bogey of Elizabethan drama. From the point of view of tragic structure, what Machiavelli was doing was destroying the integrity of tragedy by obliterating the difference between the order-figure and the rebel-figure. Machiavelli comes into Marlowe's *Jew of Malta* to speak the prologue, and there he asks: "What right had Caesar to the empire?"—in itself surely a fair enough question, and one which expresses the central issue in the tragedy of order. . . .

In Shakespeare and his contemporaries what commands loyalty is a specific social order embodied in a specific person. In the histories there is no conception of any loyalty broader than England, and even when Shakespeare's subject is the Roman Empire in which Stoicism grew up, loyalties are still concrete and personal. It is a *comitatus* group that gathers around both Caesar and Antony. In the tragedies, as in the comedies, Shakespeare's settings are deliberately archaic. The form of society in them is closer to that of the Iliad, or of *Beowulf,* than it is to ours—or to his own. The social unit involved may be a great kingdom—England or France or the Roman Empire—but its head and eyes, to use images very frequently employed, are the ruler and his small select band of personal followers. Warfare, again, continually breaks down into the warfare of the Iliad: physical prowess by individual heroes fighting in pairs. Coriolanus has no sense whatever of what Ulysses calls "the still and mental parts" of battle: he simply dashes in and fights with his own hands. The histories ignore the more realistic side of mediaeval warfare, the side that was essentially a ransom racket. The collapse of this sense of personal heroism, as in Achilles' murder of Hector or Octavius' contemptuous refusal of Antony's challenge, indicates the subsiding of the tragic into the ironic vision. The role of religion also is Homeric. Prayer in Homer consists mainly of reminding the gods pointedly that they have been well fed by a hero's sacrifices, and that victory in battle is the obvious way of making sure that the supply does not fail. Similarly, the God of Shakespeare's histories ignores the pleas of the afflicted, but appears to respond eagerly to Henry's suggestion that he will do "more" than the two chantries he has already built for King Richard's soul if he wins Agincourt.

Brutus in *Julius Caesar* is something of a Stoic, even though it is Cassius who calls himself one, and Brutus is one of the few characters in Shakespeare capable of an impersonal loyalty. But Brutus is utterly lost in the Elizabethan Rome that Shakespeare depicts. He assumes that the process of leadership looks after itself, and that his only task is to remove the danger of tyranny. Consequently he is helpless in the face of Antony, who understands the principle of personal leadership. Cassius, in contrast, is motivated in his hatred of Caesar by personal feelings; because they are personal they are concrete, and because they are concrete he can see clearly what has to be done to consolidate power. But he is emotionally dependent on Brutus: that is, his loyalties, like his resentments, are personal, and Brutus is the one man for whom personal loyalties are inappropriate. Enobarbus in *Antony and Cleopatra* shows the existential nature of tragedy even more clearly. He attempts a kind of intellectual detachment that would rationalize his leaving a losing cause and joining one that seems more in accord with the laws of nature and the general good of humanity. After all, nobody can think of Mark Antony as the Lord's anointed. But Enobarbus' own nature and humanity are bound up with his personal loyalty to Antony and to Cleopatra—for it is only when Cleopatra seems about to betray Antony that he gives in to his impulse to desert. Once he has exchanged a loyalty of experience for a loyalty of rational conviction, however, and compares his detachment with Antony's generosity, he is too numbed even to feel like a traitor. He feels simply that he is no longer alive, and he does not have to kill himself: he merely lies down and dies. . . .

In Shakespearean tragedy, man is not really man until he has entered what is called a social contract, when he ceases to be a "subject" in the philosophical sense and becomes a subject in the political one, essentially related to his society. The ordered society in Shakespeare is, to use Heidegger's term, ecstatic: its members are outside themselves, at work in the world, and their being is their function. As we saw, the vital thread of Enobarbus' life was the tie that bound him to Antony, not anything inside himself. What Falstaff sardonically notes of the relation of Shallow to his servants could in other contexts be quite seriously true: "Their spirits are so married in conjunction with the participation of society that they flock together in consent, like so many wild-geese." In the first part of *Henry VI,* Talbot, the hero of the play, is kidnapped by a French Countess, who says to him:

> Long time thy shadow hath been thrall to me,
> For in my gallery thy picture hangs:
> But now the substance shall endure the like,
> And I will chain these legs and arms of thine.

Talbot tells her that in seizing him she still has only the shadow, for "his substance, sinews, arms and strength" consist of the soldiers who follow him.

It follows that, for the leader, there is no difference between reality and appearance, between what he is and what he seems to be. His reality is his appearance, and what he does is what he is. Machiavelli remarks that it is not important that a prince should be virtuous, only that he should seem so. Until we stop to think about it, it is difficult to realize how far this principle goes in Shakespeare. Edward IV was the first to stab Prince Edward on the field of Tewkesbury, and he condemned his brother Clarence to death out of a superstitious fear of his name, influenced by his mistress. Yet, had it not been for the villainy of Gloucester, Edward would have got away with what is practically a saint's death, mourned by his faithful queen. The piety of Henry VI, on the other hand, was genuine, and therefore contemptible, because it prevented him from being a sufficiently ruthless ruler.

The prince is a *dramatic* figure: like the actor, he is required not so much to be as to appear, to put on a show. The conception of reputation in Shakespeare is bound up with the emphasis on appearance. It seems selfish for Hamlet to prevent Horatio's suicide, not because he cares about Horatio's life, but because he wants somebody to survive to tell his story properly. It seems weak in Othello, as Eliot says, to beg that a story of his killing an anti-Venetian Turk should be told about him. It seems cowardly for Cleopatra to be motivated to suicide, and Macbeth to his final hopeless fight with Macduff, out of a fear of being publicly ridiculed. But for successful rulers, how they appear in society is their real existence, and it is natural that a sense of an original function should appear like a mirage to these tragic figures in the last moments of their isolation and failure. At the end of *Hamlet* we get a strong feeling that the play we are watching is, in a sense, Horatio's story, and this feeling links together the two conceptions of reputation as the real personality and of the actor as the real man.

The good ruler is not, clearly, the ruler who performs good acts, but the ruler who does what has to be done at the time. The word "time" is very important here, and we shall return to it. Ruling involves a good deal of killing and executing, assaulting other countries when they are in a weak spot, committing minor injustices for the sake of greater ends. *De jure* authority is of little importance without *de facto* power, and the basis of *de facto* power is the ordeal by battle, the symbol of which appears at the beginning of *Richard II* in connection with Bolingbroke. The good ruler, in short, is the ruler who wins his battles. *Henry V* is a very complex play, but all its complexities do not eliminate from it the simple-minded glorification of the victory of Agincourt, and the conquest of France. It is in the exhilaration of this victory that England, in all its history, comes nearest to feeling its social identity. The feeling seems to depend on two elements to be found only on a battlefield: the presence of death and the inspiring power of enmity. In contrast to hatred, which is divisive, enmity is a socially unifying force. Two servants in *Coriolanus* agree that while war creates enmity, it is peace that breeds hatred, because then "men have less need for another," and one thinks of Falstaff's chilling phrase about the men he recruits: "the cankers of a calm world and a long peace." The leader who has the authority to expose his followers to death is the leader who commands loyalty. Timon tries to build up a peaceful society on a basis of equality, generosity, and mutual friendship, and sees it instantly disintegrate in front of him.

In the Folio text of *Julius Caesar,* Caesar makes a vague boast that he "doth not wrong": what he originally said, according to Ben Jonson, was: "Caesar did never wrong, but with just cause." Jonson thought this ridiculous, but the fact that one may do wrong with just cause is central to the whole paradox of ruling, and it is highly characteristic of Shakespeare's Caesar that he had the insight to see this. For Shakespeare's Caesar was in a position to answer Machiavelli's question in Marlowe about his right to the empire. The answer is not the simple one that might is right, but still less is it the idealistic one that might imitates right. The ruler is not, like the judge, a mere incarnation of law: he is a personality, and in tragedy the personality takes precedence over whatever is conceptual or moral. If we start with the view that the head of the state should be an instrument of law or a philosopher-king, we shall end with disillusioned reflections about the little wisdom with which the world is governed. In Shakespeare's histories and tragedies the world is not governed by wisdom at all, but by personal will. For Shakespeare's order-figures it would be more accurate to say that right imitates might. The process of holding power, however ruthless, is primary; whatever order and justice and stability there may be follow after that.

It is easy to infer from all this that Shakespeare was a great "believer" in personal rule, and wanted his audience to believe in it too: that he idealized strong rulers and minimized their faults, glorified the successful military leader and admired ruthlessness and hardness. The Roman leaders are much more attractive in him than they are in Plutarch. One could quote a good deal in support of this thesis and still misinterpret the poet. The poet presents a vision of society: the critic, in trying to interpret the vision, is almost compelled to translate it into a conception or theory of society. As a theory of society, what we have been expounding sounds rather childish, especially to people who, like ourselves, live in a post-tragic age. For us, to put a personal loyalty above a loyalty of principle, as the Nazis did, is culturally regressive: it begins in hysteria and ends in psychosis. But Shakespeare has no theory of society: what he has is a vision of society, and that vision is so powerfully convincing that we accept it without question. We often think of Shakespeare's tragedies as reflecting the social facts of his own age, but, as already indicated, they do this only to a very limited extent. The settings of *King Lear, Macbeth, Hamlet, Coriolanus* are primitive by Elizabethan standards too, and because they are primitive they are archetypal, reflecting the immutable facts of passion and power and loyalty and absurdity that are always present in human life. The vision in Shakespeare's tragedies is, quite simply, a tragic vision, a vision in which death is the end of all action, and in which the actions that lead most directly to death are the strongest ones. The wise man, says Socrates the philosopher, will live by the laws of the just state whatever state he is living in. Every man, says the tragic dramatist, lives, or would like to live, by the self-destroying passions that are most clearly revealed in the archaic settings of Shakespeare's tragedies.

In the three plays that are typically tragedies of order, the order-figure is murdered fairly soon. Hamlet's father is killed before the play begins; Duncan just as he is about to enjoy some of the fruits of victory; Caesar just before he accepts the kingship and enters into his *de jure* heritage. No actual ruler is outside the operation of the wheel of fortune, and no triumph therefore can be without its reminders of death. The Ides of March come for Caesar; Duncan is saved from the treachery of the Thane of Cawdor by the Thane's more treacherous successor; and on the great day of the senior Hamlet's life, when he won his duel with the King of Norway and Prince Hamlet was born, the first grave-digger entered into his occupation. But the simple irony of fortune's turning wheel is not the real dramatic point of these assassinations. Critics who have noted that Aristotle's word "hamartia" is also the ordinary New Testament word for sin have often assumed that a tragic victim must have a "flaw" or a "proud mind" that will make his death morally intelligible. But the flaw of the murdered ruler is simply to be there, and his proud mind is merely to be what he is. Unlike Edward IV, who imprisoned his brother because his name began with G, Caesar dismisses the warning soothsayer as a "dreamer." Caesar's "flaw," then, is only that he fails to be a superstitious tyrant. As for pride of mind, even Caesar hardly has that in an excessive degree, much less the "meek" Duncan. The fall of the prince may have a moral cause, but the cause is not primary: what is primary is the event. Or rather, not only the event, but the event along with its consequences. The important thing about the order-figure, in short, is not that he gets murdered, but that he *has been* murdered. The essential tragic action starts just after his death.

Brutus and the End of the Play

by Hugh M. Richmond

Brutus fails altogether to evolve during the action of the play. To the last he remains convinced, like most dogmatic moralists, that it is the perfection of the will that constitutes the consummation of all human endeavor:

> There is a tide in the affairs of men,
> Which, taken at the flood, leads on to fortune;
> Omitted, all the voyage of their life
> Is bound in shallows and miseries.
> On such a full sea are we now afloat;
> And we must take the current when it serves,
> Or lose our ventures. (IV. iii. 218–24)

Because he interprets all actions in personal philosophical terms, he acts somewhat at random in political terms—and almost always prematurely. Thus Antony is astonished by his opponents' surrender of their strategic mountain vantage-points in the interest merely of precipitating a decision. In this matter, as later in the matter of detailed battle tactics, Cassius is bitterly aware of the justice of Titinius' criticism: "Brutus gave the word too early" (V. iii. 5).

There is thus a supreme irony in the last scene of the play, which definitively eliminates the possibility of treating Brutus as a tragic hero, and requires instead that we see the action as a study of political forces. Brutus approaches his own suicide with complacent equanimity, because of his pride in that innocent ability to arouse loyalty that had made him so natural an instrument for conspiracy:

> Countrymen,
> My heart doth joy that yet in all my life
> I found no man but he was true to me.

"Brutus and the End of the Play." From Shakespeare's Political Plays *by Hugh M. Richmond (New York: Random House, Inc., 1967), pp. 215–17.*

I shall have glory by this losing day
More than Octavius and Mark Antony
By this vile conquest shall attain unto. (V. v. 33–38)

This is simply nonsense: Mark Antony not only shook Brutus' blood-stained hand and then went on to betray him, but he will yet become one of the most famous of Roman generals. Similarly, Octavius, as Caesar Augustus, will become not only the most distinguished of Rome's leaders, but also architect of one of the pinnacles of European cultural achievement, celebrated in the poetry of Virgil, Ovid, and Horace. It is this magnificent but unpredictable consummation of a relentless historical progression that Brutus has naively and fatally set himself against.

There is also a final and calculated deflection that is implicit in Shakespeare's assigning the resonant eulogy of the dead Brutus to Antony, who had previously so skillfully discredited the moral status that Brutus has assumed for himself. It may be true that:

All the conspirators save only he
Did what they did in envy of great Caesar;
He only, in general honest thought
And common good to all, made one of them. (V. v. 69–72)

Nevertheless, it was Brutus who made the murder feasible by his participation; and, without significantly delaying the empire, he ensured its birth in the midst of even more protracted violence and anarchy than would have been the case if Caesar had lived. Thus, in exaggerating Caesar's loss of flexibility before his death, Shakespeare's intent would appear to be to suggest, not the validity of Brutus' political diagnosis that violence was called for, but the far deeper truth that well-meant violence, even in acute political crisis, only inflames the crisis further. If there is a moral to the play, it is a harsh anticipation of Edith Cavell's severe aphorism: not simply that "Patriotism is not enough," but the even more searching thought: "Sincerity is not enough."

Julius Caesar and Revenge Tragedy

by Norman Rabkin

From the moment of the murder Brutus is marked as victim, and historical process will operate on the principle that blood will have blood. Morality is irrelevant. The efficient avenger must dissemble, disclaiming the very rhetoric he employs, urging indiscriminate mischief to take what course it will because the only way back to rest is through the spilling of blood. And because morality is irrelevant, the high principles on which the noblest of the conspirators moved become a mockery. Mark Antony is deeply and movingly touched by the death of his friend, but his responsive action is utterly without the lofty end of Brutus' bloody act. The principle of his action is opportunism. Where we know the populace to be "blocks, . . . stones, . . . worse than senseless things" (I. i. 40), he can appeal, as Brutus never deigned to do, to their vanity: "You are not wood, you are not stones, but men" (III. ii. 147). Whereas Brutus hesitates to kill Caesar despite what he takes to be an immediate danger to Rome, and refuses (however foolishly) to kill Antony himself, Mark Antony damns with a spot his sister's son, only to please a fellow triumvir for whom he has utter contempt. The point is clear. By committing an act that makes possible the dialectic of the revenge play, Brutus has automatically removed from history the feasibility of that high-minded governance to which he dedicates his life. Because of his crime against established order, success will now go to the calculating. In such a world as he has made possible, one's chances for survival are in direct proportion to one's skill at seizing the main chance; moral passion is of no value. And so as *Julius Caesar* closes it is not even the hot-blooded Antony, but the icily opportunistic Octavius who inherits Brutus' followers and makes the final disposition.

"Julius Caesar *and Revenge Tragedy." From* Shakespeare and the Common Understanding *by Norman Rabkin (New York: The Free Press, 1967), pp. 116–19.*

As he was to do, though witn a difference, in *Hamlet,* and unlike his predecessors, Shakespeare used revenge tragedy to create the moral universe, the philosophical base, of his play. In the world of *Julius Caesar,* the conventions establish a dramatically convincing representation of a universe, governed by inexorable law, in which events are brought about not according to man's idealistic intentions but deterministically by their own logic. The ghost stalking Brutus at Philippi calls up a cosmic order in which Brutus' wishful planning is totally irrelevant. "Indeed," the sage Cicero has warned us at the outset, "it is a strange-disposed time:/ But men may construe things after their fashion,/ Clean from the purpose of the things themselves" (I. iii. 33–35). Caesar's superstition, his trust of his own personal majesty, his willing self-deception, and Brutus' naïve idealism, speciously leading him to the fatal sparing of Antony as well as to the unwarranted killing of Caesar, are signs of such construing, answered finally by the irrefutable truth of historical fact played out in time. The lover, the lunatic, and the poet, Shakespeare has told us, see to the truth of things by the tricks of strong imagination, supplying through inner vision the sense and purpose that the seeing eye cannot provide. In the world of ancient history, he clearly implies, such vision is worse than futile. Troilus may argue that things are as they are valued, but Hector's contention that value lies not in the will but in the fact is confirmed by a world in which Cressida is what time proves her to be, not what Troilus posits her to be. Richard II may dream of the divinity that hedges a king, but Bolingbroke wins a crown because he understands political reality and acts only on what the moment offers.

Such a world, in which history, not man, is the determining force, is enunciated by Brutus when he erroneously uses his perception to justify battle at Philippi;

> There is a tide in the affairs of men,
> Which, taken at the flood, leads on to fortune;
> Omitted, all the voyage of their life
> Is bound in shallows and in miseries.
> On such a full sea are we now afloat;
> And we must take the current when it serves,
> Or lose our ventures. (IV. iii. 218–24)

The ironic fact that Brutus is wrong about the particular application of his insight serves only to support his generalization. His wisdom here is undercut only by his failure to realize that the flood cannot be gauged by the reasoning mind. In a world governed by necessity, plans, whether noble or otherwise, have little effect on the course of events. Brutus and Cassius believe that history is amenable to reason. Cassius' intuitions may tend to be more accurate and his plans more successful in the short range, but in the long range both men succumb to a historical process over which they have no control, while success, as we have seen, goes to the opportunist who does not plan but irresponsibly allows mischief to take its own course, and from him to Octavius, who initiates no action but simply waits to gather the fallen fruit.

Making his point in yet another way, Shakespeare shows us that even the man who attempts to live by reason is governed by irrational elements within himself that he cannot recognize. Thus the great soliloquy in which Brutus contemplates the killing of Caesar begins with a decision already made—"It must be by his death"—and proceeds through a set of rationalizations that reveal the utter absence of foundation for Brutus' fears. The proud and independent Brutus —like the proud and independent Caesar subject, as we have seen, to skillful flattery—bases his action as much on the shrewd innuendo of Cassius as on the formulations of his own reason, and, noble though he is, shows by the eve of Philippi a degeneration—manifest in his querulousness, his new eagerness to finance his campaign with ill-got money as long as he has not raised the money himself, and his exaggerated priggishness with the newly sympathetic Cassius—which demonstrates clearly that even character is determined more by process than by abiding and shaping inner principles.

Brutus' ultimate wisdom, the only statement he ever makes to which the play offers no contradictory answer, is his recognition that the end is known only when the day has ended. Significantly this realization brings him precisely to Caesar's position: Death, the necessary end, will come when it will come. In the fact, not men's construing, is the meaning. Man is only actor, not playwright, and as actor he may not even, in the terms of *Juluis Caesar,* know the conventions of the play in which he acts. In Cassius' ebullient words as the conspirators bend over the body of Caesar, Shakespeare makes mortifyingly explicit the fundamental irony of his tragedy:

> Stoop, then, and wash. How many ages hence
> Shall this our lofty scene be acted over
> In states unborn and accents yet unknown! (III. i. 111–13)

But by this point Shakespeare has made us party to his irony: He has let us see and consider before the assassination the identity between Caesar and Brutus which is at the center of the play. Confronted with a body of historical material which meant a great many things to a great many people, yet characteristically motivated by the artist's desire to transform the raw materials of historiography into the coherent form of significant art, Shakespeare has experimented with both structure and convention in *Julius Caesar*. By creating virtually *ex nihilo* a surprising parallelism between two crucial scenes, and by turning at its climax what promised to be a tragical history into a revenge play, he has twice directed our responses toward the meaning that is the vital principle of the play.

Julius Caesar: "The Specialty of Rule"

by William and Barbara Rosen

When *Julius Caesar* was performed in 1599, Elizabethans must have seen in its events their own uncertainties about a sudden change of rule and its possible consequences. Elizabeth was over sixty-five, a painted old woman living on a parody of flattery that had once been sincere. Her subjects knew that she was beginning to fail, but they had no idea of what was to come next, for there was no heir, and the Queen would name none. Once again there might be a disputed succession, the overriding dread of the time. It is striking that Shakespeare, turning from *Henry V* (1599), began to write not the "history" but the "tragedy" of *Julius Caesar,* perhaps finding in the civil wars that followed the death of an aging ruler some reflections of the horrors that could overtake his own country, and seeing in the complexities of a power struggle the problems for his own government.

The beginning of *Julius Caesar* shows the fickleness of popular opinion: the citizens are celebrating the triumph of Caesar, whereas only a short time before they wholeheartedly supported Pompey. Having overcome and slain Pompey, Caesar rides high on the Wheel of Fortune; but as the action progresses, the populace shifts allegiances with shifting fortunes. When Brutus speaks after the death of Caesar, the response is: "Let him be Caesar." After hearing Antony speak, the people switch their affection to "noble Antony," and want to "burn the house of Brutus." In the historical story of Julius Caesar the issue is between two forms of government, absolute monarchy and a republic. But the concept of a republic was alien to Elizabethan England, and Shakespeare utterly discounts either its possibility or desirability in his play. Departing from Plutarch, his main source, he makes the central characters much more surely in command of events than in fact they were. The Roman Senate, with its system

---

Julius Caesar: *"The Specialty of Rule" by William and Barbara Rosen. First published here, by permission of the authors.*

of debate and voting, is left completely out of the picture; we get, instead, a subservient Parliament as background for the conspirators. Not particularly interested in the intricacies of Roman politics, Shakespeare concentrates on the ability of various leaders to hold power; less concerned with heroes and villains than with styles of public life that demonstrate qualities of leadership, he shows how men act, and how they are then forced to contend with the unexpected results of action.

The unexpected shifts in political action often require that strategies of public policy have a kind of moral flexibility which appears as mere opportunism in private life. Elizabeth's policy, for example, was so pragmatic that it is impossible to discover in its workings her personal beliefs. She used paid informers, spies, and *agents provocateurs.* The graceless convolutions of her policy kept Europe guessing; her meanness drove her most faithful public servants into debt and despair. Yet few doubted that her most squalid devices were subordinate to an extraordinary sense of statesmanship. The necessary was always done, though seldom elegantly or morally; the results of action were always dealt with on their own merits.

Because the royal position was unchallengeable in Elizabethan thinking about the nature of things, the King could act without regard to personal advancement; his least pleasing acts could therefore be free of self-interest. In *Richard II,* however, we see the problem of the "evil" king; there is a discrepancy between the office and the man who fills it, and yet, no matter how bad the king, rebellion can never be excused: it may seem essential, but it is, at best, a "necessary evil" for which the revolutionary, like a Greek tragic hero, incurs guilt and punishment. Henry IV can never wear Richard's crown in peace. Plagued by rebellion, and tormented by the thought that his son, Hal, is not only unworthy, but ambitious for the crown, he accepts his troubles as divine punishment for his own rebellion against Richard. His death, he tells his son, will remove the curse from the crown, "for what in me was purchased/ Falls upon thee in a more fairer sort,/ So thou the garland wear'st successively." As Henry V could succeed to rule without sin, but not his father, who won the throne by eliminating a legitimate ruler, so Octavius can succeed, but not the conspirators.

Because there is no kingship in *Julius Caesar* and God has therefore no representative in the system of government, Fortune (in public affairs) is not bound to the service of divine order, and her changes are everywhere apparent. There are not many plays in which events are so patently determined by slight miscalculations, mistakes of judgment, wrong "hunches," flawless logic applied to the wrong problem, or misplaced outbreaks of emotion warping decisions. Intention is continually frustrated by event. Actions produce results that are quite different from the ones which had been planned. It is possible that Plutarch's narrative technique provides another explanation for the emotional ambivalence of *Julius Caesar* (as well as Shakespeare's other Roman plays). In striving for fullness and accuracy of assessment, Plutarch shifts from a favorable account of a character's traits and actions to an unfavorable point of view and back again with a startling abruptness, and usually refuses a final judgment. We are left with a number of viewpoints or, as in the *Comparisons,* with a collection of likenesses and differences that often lead to a curious kind of double vision, particularly in the comparisons of one character with another.

Our estimation of the characters and events of *Julius Caesar* is liable to shift according to our viewpoint: if we react according to our personal sympathies, Brutus is more likable than a superstitious, vain Caesar; if we consider public consequences, Brutus is far less commendable because he brings to Rome chaos and injustice, not "Peace, freedom, and liberty!" He kills only a man, not the spirit of Caesar, which comes back to haunt him at Sardis and Philippi, and finally to triumph, in the person of Octavius Caesar.

The play demands more than a partial response; it asks that we judge a man not only for what he is but what he does. Consequences are no less important than intentions; we see that well-meaning is no guarantee of well-doing, and that bad things done for a good cause, or by people who think themselves good, are still bad. But not to do the bad things which government sometimes requires is also disastrous—witness the public failures of Brutus. Although virtue guides the civilized conduct of individuals, in this play the shifting concerns of public action, governed by necessity, demand more pragmatic laws. There are no easy solutions to the dilemmas and ironies that result.

Caesar shows great strength as the "constant," disinterested ruler who will not give in to the private entreaties of an Artemidorus or Cimber; he is also superstitious, and can be led by flattery. Both implacability and weakness contribute to his downfall. The envious Cassius belittles Caesar for not being as physically strong as he, yet in the practical matters of power politics he is emotionally unable to stand against Brutus, of whose moral qualities he is in awe. Brutus can kill Caesar to prevent tyranny, yet he cannot safeguard the deed by eliminating Antony as well, nor can he strengthen his cause by resorting to forced loans to finance his army. He will neither abdicate judgment in favor of the practical advice of Cassius nor bow to the necessary compromises of strategy and power. His moral strength is paradoxically the source of his weakness in the public world; indeed, the public pursuit of private virtue turns out to be the worst kind of self-indulgence. Antony, in contrast, brilliantly uses every political trick there is, and can barter human lives without a qualm. Yet he genuinely lacks ambition; his aim is simple revenge for Caesar's death, and nothing more constructive. He steps aside at the first brush with the purposeful Octavius, and abdicates decision and final authority without protest.

While there are conflicting traits in Julius Caesar's personality, they do not cancel out and render him ineffective as a ruler. He "is superstitious grown of late"; but when it comes to deciding whether or not to go to the Senate, he finally discounts omens and forebodings in favor of a decision that Calphurnia's dream is "all amiss interpreted," and that to take notice of it might cause the image of an over-concerned husband to obscure that of an unshakable Caesar who is fit to be offered supreme rule. He chooses the act that suits the position of Caesar.

Comprehending an impersonal justice, Caesar is able to represent it. He refuses his dearest friend's petition for Publius Cimber's pardon because the appeal is purely emotional and personal. He can not give in because he is

> constant as the Northern Star,
> Of whose true-fixed and resting quality
> There is no fellow in the firmament.

Many interpret this stance just before the assassination to be a last manifestation of arrogance that justifies the conspirators' action, forgetting that if it is arrogance in a man to claim "unshaked" constancy, it is necessary for a ruler to possess it.

In an extraordinary speech rationalizing an impending assassination (II. i. 10–34), Brutus acknowledges that Caesar is an impartial administrator of justice: "I have not known when his affections swayed/ More than his reason." In order to kill friend, benefactor, and ruler, Brutus must wrap himself in a cause. A divinely appointed king is his own cause; he does what is necessary to safeguard himself because he knows that his office is necessary to the state; and, like Henry V, he has no qualms about executing traitors. But a rebel or assassin must act as the representative of something larger than himself, otherwise planned murder becomes impossible. *Othello* dramatizes the process of making a cause: first, the object of hatred must be "proved" to be inordinately vicious and unfit to live; second, the killer must see himself as the agent of Justice, as an impersonal executioner purging the world of evil.

Cassius "proves" Caesar to be physically inferior: the man, bested in a swimming contest, had to be rescued from the water; in Spain, he suffered from fever. Brutus, too intelligent for this sort of rationalization, justifies himself by a kind of intellectual geometry full of unknowns: let Caesar desire to be king; a king is a tyrant in embryo because absolute power corrupts absolutely; therefore, Caesar is ambitious to be a tyrant; "Then lest he may, prevent." Brutus is too noble-spirited to denigrate Caesar as he is, but he has the dangerous advantage of coming from an aristocratic family, whose tradition of public service is in itself a ready-made cause; he has a clearly defined function in the state: a Brutus kills tyrants. Because the aristocratic tradition of this kind is inevitably geared to the maintenance of the *status quo,* Brutus fears a future which may be different, and can only see his actions as guaranteeing that once the danger is eliminated, the future will obediently fall back into the pattern of the past without further effort. His thought passes easily from what has been to what will be, and he can then resolve to kill Caesar, the future tyrant. Duty calls him to be the future liberator of Rome; but the interim is difficult, for daily life strives to drag him out of his dream of historical necessity into the real present where Caesar is just, and he is Caesar's friend.

Once the deed is done, both Cassius and Brutus can see it as an already inevitable part of history, the subject of plays which justify and praise them as saviors of their country—

Cassius. How many ages hence
Shall this our lofty scene be acted over
In states unborn and accents yet unknown?
Brutus. How many times shall Caesar bleed in sport,
That now on Pompey's basis lies along
No worthier than the dust!
Cassius. So oft as that shall be,

So often shall the knot of us be called
The men that gave their country liberty.

It takes the ominous, heavily stressed lines of Antony's servant to bring Cassius and Brutus back to their real situation. They do not get a chance to act out what they had planned, the role of liberators, which called for the highly theatrical waving of red weapons over their heads, and the crying out in the streets, "Peace, freedom, and liberty!" It is not surprising that Antony quickly takes command of what is going on, and it is soon evident that of all those who assume power, Brutus is the least equipped for action in the public world.

A ruler with a "public personality" is able to stand clear of his own confused, personal desires and plans, as well as those of others. Caesar could do this. Brutus could never cut free of his moral and aristocratic inheritance; Cassius, of his hatred of Caesar and love of Brutus. Once Antony starts acting independently after Caesar's death, he moves successfully every time; though his deeds are bloody and brutal, they achieve the desired short-term results. Antony is free but anarchic; he has not the compulsive desire for political order which provides stable, absolute rule. Octavius acquiesces in the proscriptions; however, by an unexpected show of strength just before Philippi, he assumes command. When battle is over, Octavius is able to start clear, unhampered by the tangled wills of enemies and supporters. The man who assumes rule is the man who has been least entangled; like Caesar, though he is no king, he has the aura of one fated to rule; unlike the others, he has not overtly maneuvered or contrived for position; it has come to him by providence and inheritance.

In the absence of a natural leader who can control events strongly enough to make history, not merely endure it, every action offers a series of open options, an unending procession of ambiguous choices —and perhaps that is why *Julius Caesar* is above all a play of ambiguities and alternatives. The noblest Roman of them all fails miserably in everything but the form of his intent, and brings actual ruin and injustice by trying to forestall them. The triumvirs who arbitrarily select their relatives for death are a kind of nightmare projection of the tyranny Brutus feared might grow from Caesar's kingship. The vain, superstitious Caesar correctly feared Cassius and the omens; but he did not act to forestall his fears. Flavius and Marullus were "put to silence" for insulting Caesar the ruler; no one

—not even Cassius—suffers because he seems a threat to Caesar the man.

Without an office that ensures justice, public life becomes the web of conflicting virtues and vices that we see after Caesar's death. At the end we are left with a military leader who is efficient but unsympathetic; indeed, Shakespeare's successful, impersonal rulers—Henry V, Octavius Caesar—appear as colorless men who, having integrated or eliminated conflicting emotions, are cold and calculating, more like impersonal institutions than individuals whose energy and appeal come from a conflict of allegiances. However, as *Julius Caesar* demonstrates, people of high ideals and good intentions are *too* emotional; ambition has never taught them the facts of public life, and they cannot make events obey them. The dilemma is simple but profound, and in our time is again reduced to its barest terms—anarchy or tyranny; and it plays itself out as it did in the Capitol, but not on a stage, and with real blood.

Chronology of Important Dates

	Shakespeare	*The Age*
1558		Accession of Queen Elizabeth I.
1564	Shakespeare born at Stratford-upon-Avon; baptized April 26.	Marlowe born.
1572		Jonson and Donne born.
1576		James Burbage built the permanent playhouse in England, named the Theater, in the suburbs north of London. Marston born.
1582	Shakespeare married to Anne Hathaway.	
1583–85	Susanna and the twins, Hamnet and Judith, born.	
1587		*The Spanish Tragedy* by Thomas Kyd. Marlowe's *Tamburlaine,* Part I.
1589		*Jew of Malta.*
1591–92	The three *Henry VI* plays; *The Comedy of Errors.*	
1592		Marlowe's *Doctor Faustus* and *Edward II.*
1593–94	*Venus and Adonis* and *The Rape of Lucrece* dedicated to the Earl of Southampton. *Titus Andronicus; The Taming of the Shrew; Richard III; Two Gentlemen of Verona.* Shakespeare joined in forming the Lord Chamberlain's company of actors.	Marlowe killed. Kyd dies.

1595–96	*A Midsummer Night's Dream; Richard II; Romeo and Juliet; King John; The Merchant of Venice.* The death of Hamnet.	
1597–98	The two parts of *Henry IV; Much Ado about Nothing.* Shakespeare purchased New Place in Stratford.	Jonson's *Every Man in his Humour.*
1599–1600	*As You Like It; Henry V; Julius Caesar; Twelfth Night; The Merry Wives of Windsor.* Shakespeare's company moved to the new Globe Theater.	*The Shoemakers' Holiday* (1599) by Thomas Dekker. Marston's *Antonio and Mellida.* Jonson's *Everyman Out of his Humour.*
1601–2	*Hamlet; All's Well that Ends Well; Troilus and Cressida.*	Jonson's *The Poetaster* (1601) and the so-called "War of the Theaters." The abortive rebellion of the Earl of Essex.
1603–4	*Measure for Measure; Othello.* Shakespeare's company became the King's Men.	(1603) The death of Elizabeth and the accession of James I. Jonson's *Sejanus.*
1605–6	*Macbeth; King Lear.*	*Volpone* by Ben Jonson (1606)
1607–8	*Antony and Cleopatra; Timon of Athens; Coriolanus; Pericles.*	
1610	*Cymbeline.* The King's Men acquired the Blackfriars Playhouse.	
1610–11	*The Winter's Tale, The Tempest.* Shakespeare retired to Stratford.	*The Alchemist* (1610) by Ben Jonson.
1616	Shakespeare died, April 23.	
1623	The First Folio edition of Shakespeare's plays.	

Notes on the Editor and Contributors

LEONARD F. DEAN, editor of this volume, is Professor of English at New York University. His publications include studies of Shakespeare, Erasmus, More, and Bacon.

GEOFFREY BULLOUGH is Professor of English Language and Literature, King's College, University of London. He has been very active as an editor and critic, especially on seventeenth-century subjects.

SIGURD BURCKHARDT (1916–1966) was educated in German primary and secondary schools and at the University of California (B.A., 1940, M.A., 1945) and Ohio State University (Ph.D., 1956). He taught at St. Mary's College, Ohio State University, and the University of California, San Diego, where he was Professor of German Literature at the time of his death. He was a distinguished translator, and published widely on Goethe, Kleist, and Shakespeare. His essays on Shakespeare have been collected as *Shakespearean Meanings* to be published by Princeton University Press.

MAURICE CHARNEY is Professor of English at Rutgers University. His publications include a collection of essays on Shakespeare's Roman plays.

DAVID DAICHES, Professor of English at the University of Sussex, is well known on both sides of the Atlantic as a wide-ranging critic and man of letters.

R. A. FOAKES is Professor of English at the University of Kent and has published widely on Renaissance subjects.

NORTHROP FRYE is University Professor of English at the University of Toronto. He is perhaps best known for *Anatomy of Criticism,* but he has published widely and is one of the most influential of modern critics.

HARLEY GRANVILLE-BARKER (1877–1946) was a playwright and producer as well as a critic. In addition to several volumes of *Prefaces to Shakespeare,* his publications include *On Dramatic Method* and *The Companion to Shakespeare Studies* (with G. B. Harrison).

ROBERT B. HEILMAN is Professor and Chairman of English at the University of Washington. His publications include studies of *King Lear* (*This Great Stage*) and of *Othello* (*Magic in the Web*).

LEO KIRSCHBAUM was Professor of English at Wayne State University. His publications include editions of Marlowe and Spenser, *The True Text of*

King Lear, Shakespeare and the Stationers, and *Character and Characterization in Shakespeare.*

L. C. Knights, King Edward VII Professor of English Literature at the University of Cambridge, is the author of *Drama and Society in the Age of Jonson, Explorations, Some Shakespearean Themes and An Approach to Hamlet,* and other critical studies.

John Palmer (1885–1944), diplomat and man of letters, published *The Comedy of Manners, Ben Jonson,* and *The Comic Characters of Shakespeare.*

Norman Rabkin is Professor of English at the University of California, Berkeley. His publications include collections of essays on Shakespeare and Elizabethan drama.

Hugh M. Richmond, a graduate of Cambridge and Oxford, teaches at the University of California, Berkeley, and is the author of a study of the Stuart love lyric.

William Rosen, Professor of English at the University of Connecticut, is the author of *Shakespeare and the Craft of Tragedy.* He and his wife, Barbara, edited the Signet *Julius Caesar.*

Ernest Schanzer is Lecturer in English Literature at the University of Liverpool. His publications include *Shakespeare's Appian.*

Arthur Sewell, Byron Professor of English at the University of Athens, has also written on Milton and Katherine Mansfield.

Brents Stirling, Professor of English at the University of Washington, is the author of *The Populace in Shakespeare,* and many critical essays.

Mark Van Doren, emeritus Professor of English at Columbia University, is one of America's most distinguished poets and men of letters.

Selected Bibliography

T. S. Dorsch, ed. The Arden Edition of *Julius Caesar,* London, 1955. A 70-page introduction and thorough annotation.

Mildred E. Hartsock, "The Complexity of *Julius Caesar,*" *PMLA,* LXXXVI (1966), 56–62. The heart of the play is its intellectual relativism and irresolvable paradoxes.

G. Wilson Knight, "The Eroticism of *Julius Caesar,*" *The Imperial Theme,* London, 1931. Brutus sacrifices love to honor.

M. W. MacCallum, *Shakespeare's Roman Plays and Their Background,* London, 1910. Substantial, perceptive, and old-fashioned.

J. C. Maxwell, "Shakespeare's Roman Plays: 1900–1956," *Shakespeare Survey,* 10 (1957), 1–11. Useful bibliographical article.

Ann Righter, *Shakespeare and the Idea of the Play,* London, 1962. A fresh and thoughtful study of Shakespeare's theatricality.

William and Barbara Rosen, eds. The Signet Edition of *Julius Caesar,* New York, 1963. A valuable critical introduction and four essays on the play.

Gordon Ross Smith, "Brutus, Virtue, and Will," *Shakespeare Quarterly,* X (1959), 367–79. The case against Brutus.

T. J. B. Spencer, "Shakespeare and the Elizabethan Romans," *Shakespeare Survey,* 10 (1957), 27–38. Shows that Roman figures were endlessly discussed.

J. I. M. Stewart, *Character and Motive in Shakespeare,* London, 1949. Good on the two sides of Caesar.

Roy Walker, "Unto Caesar: A Review of Recent Productions," *Shakespeare Survey,* 11 (1958), 132 ff.